NEW MEXICO'S RAILROADS

NEW MEXICO'S
RAILROADS

A Historical Survey
Revised Edition
David F. Myrick

UNIVERSITY OF NEW MEXICO PRESS: *Albuquerque*

Library of Congress Cataloging-in-Publication Data

Myrick, David F.
New Mexico's railroads : an historical survey /
David F. Myrick.—Rev. ed.
p.   cm.
ISBN 0-8263-1185-7
1. Railroads—New Mexico—History. I. Title.
HE2771.N6M95   1990
385'.09789—dc20   89-27309
                                                           CIP

Design by Susan Gutnik.

CONTENTS

ACKNOWLEDGMENTS

I was scarcely seven years old when I saw New Mexico for the first time. The air was charged with excitement; it was my initial trip outside the confines of California. My parents, my brother and I were ensconced in a drawing room in the standard Pullman sleeping car of the day on the *California Limited* with Chicago as our destination. Though I was assigned to the upper berth at bedtime, the daylight hours were delightful and the pleasant memory of the wheels clicking over the rail joints of the Santa Fe tracks as I had my first practical lesson in geography in the grand open-end observation car is one that will last for a long time.

Since that time I have been in New Mexico many times for there are varied landscapes to see and many people to meet in that state. Talking with people about the past was indeed the most gratifying part of my visits and I learned much about the history of the railroads from them. Through correspondence, interviews, old records, reports, maps, newspapers and walking and riding over the land, I have gathered data on the railroads in New Mexico and Western Texas and I thank all those who assisted me in one way or another. Certain people were particularly helpful and I acknowledge their aid in the ensuing paragraphs.

From the individual railroads, many people answered my questions. Among the Santa Fe men who assisted me were E. S. Marsh, W. C. Burk, Robert Gerht, James D. Jackson and Harvey Huston of Chicago, Gil Sweet of San Francisco, C. B. Kurtz of La Junta and W. H. Crutchfield and George B. Kelley of Albuquerque. Other railroad people who provided useful information were W. J. Dixon, J. G. Pate and Esther M. Glaser of the Rock Island, G. B. Aydelott, E. Main, E. H. Waring, Jackson Thode, the late Carlton T. Sills and Lucy Evans Hahn of the Rio Grande, George Kraus and L. D. Farrar of the Southern Pacific, Harry E. Hammer of the T & P and R. J. Cunningham of the Colorado and Southern responded generously to my requests for information and photographs. Arthur L. Lloyd and Bruce Heard of Amtrak graciously supplied photographs and data for the new edition. Such people as Elaine and Joe Hodges of Denver who opened new doors for me and Lewis W. Douglas who filled me in on the EP&SW "battle of Deming" contributed much to the project.

In Santa Fe, Dr. Myra Ellen Jenkins, Mrs. Avis C. Price, L. C. White, Phil Cooke and Mrs. J. K. Shishkin provided me with information or photographs. In addition to the libraries in Santa Fe, I am indebted to the library staffs of the University of New Mexico, Denver Public Library, Colorado State Archives, U.S. Geological Survey, U.S. Bureau of Mines, The Bancroft Library and, in San Francisco, the Mechanics' Institute, California Division of Mines and Geology Library and the Sutro Library.

Information relating to lumber operations in New Mexico was obtained from J. W. Kendall, John M. Hall, John C. Keesey, E. P. Rees, Fred Coldren, U. R. Armstrong, G. F. Zimmerman, J. M. Childers, W. E. Rutherford and Fred E. Bornell.

Frank Hord and the U.S. Borax & Chemical Co. furnished data relating to potash mining and related railroads while John A. Lentz, H. E. Cooley, Harry Gunderson, Cameron Kirk supplied information concerning the important mining area of Southwestern New Mexico. Don Zoss of the Bureau of Reclamation, Lee Moore of Western Fuels Association, and John Atkins and Phil Hewlett of BPH-Utah International furnished information about contemporary coal mining in northern New Mexico.

From El Paso, I received much assistance from Chris Fox, Millard McKinney, Mrs. Dorothy J. Neal, Mrs. Virginia P. Hoke, Leon C. Metz and J. A. Davis, Jr. concerning the railroads and street car lines of that area.

Others who kindly gave of their time and knowledge included James D. Shinkle, Raymond F. Waters, Mrs. C. C. Yearwood, Norris K. Maxwell, Martin Ruoss, Charles O'Malley, Tony R. Elias, L. I. Perrigo, L. S. Wicks, John E. Southwell, Charles Stevens, C. B. Bourne, Mrs. Wesley Meng, Kaiser Steel Corporation, and Utah Construction & Mining Company.

Photographs came from many sources; most are individually acknowledged. Particular thanks should be tendered Al C. Phelps, R. H. Kindig, Fred M. Springer, Henry E. Bender, Jr., John G. Harlan, Guy Dunscomb, and Ted Wurm as well as the Santa Fe and the Southern Pacific. Locomotive technicalities were explained to me by D. S. Richter and the late S. R. Wood. To all these individuals and to many other unnamed helpers of government agencies, corporations—both mining and railroad—libraries and historical societies, my sincere thanks.

David F. Myrick
Santa Barbara
October 1989

Four months after I completed all my revisions, my attention was drawn to William Raymond Morley who, after completing his work in New Mexico, was the engineer for two railroads in Mexico affiliated with the Santa Fe. These were the Sonora Railway, which was built from Guaymas to Nogales in 1882, and the Mexican Central Railway opened from El Paso to Mexico City in 1884. On January 3, 1883, while working on the latter road in Chihuahua, Morley was killed by gunshot. The circumstances relating to his death have not been resolved; however, his grandson, Norman Cleaveland, is of the opinion that Morley was murdered as part of the cover-up of the Santa Fe Ring.

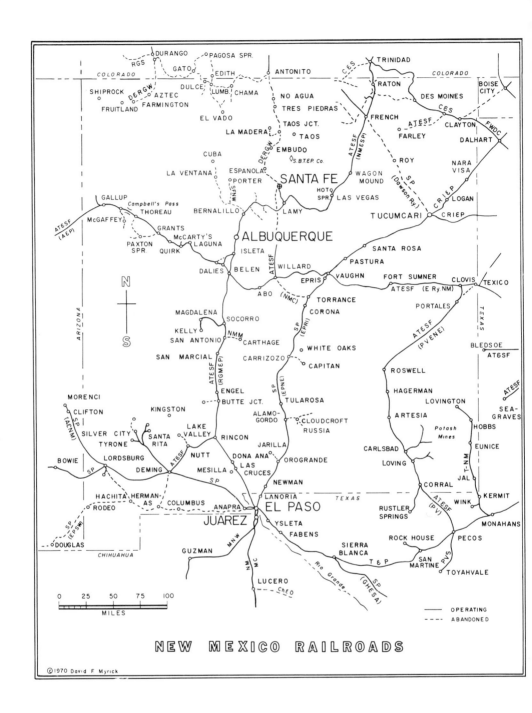

NEW MEXICO RAILROADS

OPERATING
ABANDONED

© 1970 David F. Myrick

INTRODUCTION

Early in 1912, New Mexico became the 47th state of the Union, but this late entry in no way shrinks the extended history of European discovery and settlement which predates that of many areas along the Atlantic seaboard. Santa Fe, the capital of the state, founded by the Spanish in 1610, was the objective of traders from a vast area. Journeys of the traders to and from the Missouri resulted in the Santa Fe Trail. Not surprisingly, New Mexico figured prominently in the Pacific Railroad Surveys of 1853–56, although nearly a quarter of a century was to go by before the first locomotive whistle echoed through a mountain pass leading into the territory.

Early railroad proposals were concerned with building *through* the territory while actual railroad building, measured by the number of lines, was largely for development within the borders of New Mexico. The slogan "Land of Enchantment" may have provided the stimulus to bring many visitors to this part of the Southwest in later years, but it was the unusually wide range of natural resources that brought pioneer industry, jobs, people and the short line railroads that served them. Extensive coal deposits, oil fields, potash mines, metals such as copper, zinc, lead, iron, silver and gold, agricultural and livestock lands and great stands of timber were effectively linked to markets by rail—both short lines and branches feeding to the main lines of major systems.

The number of railroads in New Mexico's history can be expanded or contracted at will depending on definitions. Most of the larger railroads were the result of a series of combinations of corporate names, often the same piece of track having a succession of legal ownerships. Of the companies owning or operating rail properties in New Mexico, the enlarged definition would probably yield a number in excess of 100. A list of railroads filing papers of incorporation in the Territorial days is almost double that number. As Texas laws for many years required that railroads operating in that state be incorporated under its laws, railroads running from El Paso into New Mexico added still more corporations to the list. Because of their significant contribution to the overall railroad history of New Mexico, railroads in Western Texas are included in this book.

Though major railroad projects such as the Atlantic and Pacific had their inception earlier, November 1, 1869 was the date of the first railroad incorporation in New Mexico. While its principal office was given as Santa Fe, the title gave no hint as to the area to be served: Mississippi Valley and Pacific Rail Road Company. One of its several proposed routes was from Gallup to Raton Pass to meet the Kansas Pacific. The promoters also had in mind a later project to follow Beal's wagon road across Arizona to meet proposed California railroads near Fort Mohave.

A few weeks later, some of the same busy people filed papers for their El Paso and Rio Gila Railroad and Telegraph Company. Projected routes included one from El Paso to Yuma, El Paso to Delaware Creek, Texas (near the southeast corner of New Mexico where the Santa Fe completed its sulphur branch in 1969), as well as a link to their other system. Great ideas were these railroads but, with no construction funds forthcoming, ideas are all they were.

More incorporations were to take place, but it was not until late in 1878 that the first railroad entered New Mexico. Steaming across the boundary at Raton Pass, the Santa Fe opened an active period of construction in New Mexico in which two other companies soon joined. By the time the Santa Fe had finished building southward through the territory to reach El Paso in June 1881, three railroads had built over 1,000 miles— all in just 30 months.

In this brief period of time when one-third of the total railroad mileage of New Mexico was built, the Santa Fe's extensions included a line to Deming to meet the Southern Pacific, thus forming the nation's second transcontinental railroad, as well as a branch to the territorial capital. Through the affiliated Atlantic and Pacific, its tracks reached westward through Gallup into Arizona on the way to California.

Also entering from the north were the narrow-gauge tracks of the Denver and Rio Grande. One line approached Santa Fe (the final link was not accomplished until 1887) while another traversed part of the lumber lands in Rio Arriba County on the way to the silver mines around Durango, Colorado.

Into the southwestern corner of New Mexico came the Southern Pacific in 1880 to continue on to Deming, then across the Rio Grande to El Paso and beyond.

Thus in a relatively short span of time, a major step in the transformation of New Mexico's mode of transportation took place. Although horse-drawn wagons were still important to the way of life of many isolated towns and would continue to be so well into the twentieth century, the steam locomotive was beginning to bring about many changes in the economy of the territory.

The balance of the decade ending in 1890 reflected little major construction insofar as New Mexico railroads were concerned, the notable exception being the driving of the last spike in the northeastern part of the territory in 1888 to mark the completion of the present Colorado and Southern Railway from Denver to Texas. El Paso, already served by railroads from three different directions, celebrated the opening of the Mexican Central from Juarez, its neighboring city just across the Rio Grande, to Chihuahua in 1882. And in that same year trains of the Texas and Pacific came into El Paso for the first time.

The general economic depression which spread across the country during the 1890s curtailed railroad developments, but some new short lines appeared in New Mexico. Continuing the

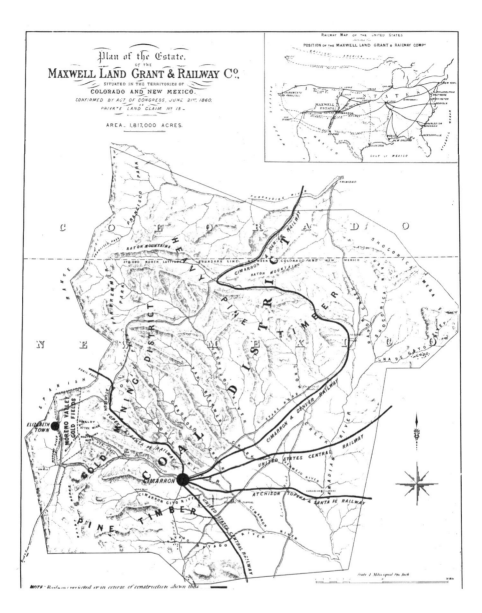

Although the fabled Maxwell Land Grant is the subject of many articles and books, little is said about the proposed railroad aspects of this enterprise or the other railroads shown on the map. Only the Atchison, Topeka & Santa Fe Railway was constructed but it never tapped Cimarron. Museum of New Mexico Collection.

trend initiated in the late 1880s, a few more lumber railroads reached out into the woods. This was also the time that tracks were laid in Pecos Valley for a road which eventually became part of the Santa Fe family.

Working intermittently between economic slumps during the first decade of this century, entrepreneurs filled out most of the railroad map of New Mexico. Col. Eddy's road, the El Paso and Northeastern, which during 1898 and 1899 had built almost 200 miles north of El Paso, continued its course to meet the Rock Island at Santa Rosa in 1902. This was also the decade that the Santa Fe opened the Belen Cutoff, a new freight route across New Mexico avoiding the heavy grades of Raton Pass.

The copper road, El Paso and Southwestern, moving eastward from Arizona, reached El Paso late in 1902; three years later it absorbed Col. Eddy's road.

Several lines were built to tap coal mines and timber lands during this decade. In addition to a line Col. Eddy built to his Dawson coal properties, the St. Louis Rocky Mountain and Pacific Railway also served coal mines and provided an outlet for the Cimarron and Northwestern Railway, a lumber carrier in Colfax County. Another independent line was the New Mexico Central which provided an alternate route to the territorial capital and added 116 miles of railroad to the total.

During these years (1901–1910), over 1,200 miles of railroad were built. In 1914, the eleven common carrier companies reporting to the State Corporation Commission of New Mexico operated 3,124 miles of railroad in New Mexico. As subsequent additions were offset by abandonments, the total common carrier mileage was held to about 3,000 miles through 1930. Winding through the woods were many more miles of lumber roads with short branches, often temporary in nature, lasting only long enough to permit cutting of a stand of timber. Other industrial spurs served coal and copper mines.

After World War I, additional mileages were generally limited to lumber roads, the most important being the Santa Fe Northwestern Railway. It was in 1924 that a major change in railroad ownership took place when the Southern Pacific acquired the system of the El Paso and Southwestern. Southeastern New Mexico welcomed its first train when the Texas–New Mexico came into Hobbs and Lovington in 1930.

In the years since the first railroad came into New Mexico, it is worthy of note that about 80% of the common carrier mileage was built in two periods: 1878–1882 and 1898–1910. At the end of 1968, there were six common carrier railroads operating 2,225 miles in New Mexico but only five a year later as the 99 miles of narrow gauge lines of the Rio Grande were abandoned. Construction of new lines still continues in the form of branch lines to serve coal or sulphur deposits. Of the industrial railroads, the last of the logging railroads disappeared some years ago along with the mining roads but, here again, new construction does occur, an example being the Phelps Dodge railroad to Tyrone, finished in 1967.

Though the railroads of the past are no longer operating, their history is not forgotten. Many people, both as individuals and in such organizations as the Rocky Mountain Railroad Club, the Colorado Railroad Museum and the Railroad Club of New Mexico, through their dedicated interests, are adding to the knowledge of the part played by railroads in Western history.

Since this book appeared in September 1970, there have been several corporate revisions; those affecting the Chicago, Rock Island and Pacific Railroad were far reaching.

Commencing in 1962, Southern Pacific began negotiations to acquire the Rock Island and soon the Union Pacific indicated its interest. As a result, agreements were reached whereby SP would acquire the Rock Island Lines south and west of Kansas City for a cash payment of $120 million while the UP would obtain the northern segment. About the same time, the Santa Fe and the Chicago and North Western Railway announced their intentions to buy and divide the property along generally similar lines except that the C&NW would own the railroad to Tucumcari and Santa Rosa.

Initial applications were filed with the ICC in 1963 seeking authority for control of various segments of the Rock Island. Hearings before the ICC, best described as "marathon," finally ended in August 1968 at which time the long wait for the Examiner's Report began. Nearly three years elapsed before the first section appeared and the final report was released in February 1973. Then it was the full Commission's turn to ponder the mountains of evidence and it issued its decision in December 1974. Certain conditions were unacceptable and, more important, the physical property of the Rock Island had deteriorated badly.

In March 1975, the Rock Island went into bankruptcy again. Subsequently, SP entered into negotiations with the trustee of the Rock Island to purchase the railroad from Santa Rosa and Tucumcari to Topeka and from Kansas City to St. Louis, as well as the Rock Island's trackage rights over the UP between Topeka and Kansas City. This time, the St. Louis Southwestern Railway (Cotton Belt), an SP subsidiary, filed the application with the ICC to acquire the segments described and, in October 1980, this became a reality. Immediately after the purchase, the segment west of Topeka was rebuilt for high-speed freight service. This required a year of work and cost almost $100 million.

All of the separately-operated railroads in Mexico were consolidated into the National Railways of Mexico in 1987. The Chino copper mines at Santa Rita, long an important Kennecott producer, changed ownership when Phelps Dodge acquired a two-thirds ownership at the end of 1986.

The Missouri Pacific System, including the Texas–New Mexico Railway, came under the control of the Union Pacific Railroad in December 1982 and was absorbed into the latter company in 1986. In the early spring of 1989, the Union Pacific contracted to sell the entire 107-mile line of the T-NM to the Austin & Northwestern Railroad, a subsidiary of RailTex, Inc., a San Antonio firm operating several railroads that formerly were branch lines of major carriers.

For many years, the CB&Q Railroad had controlled the Colorado and Southern Railway through majority stock ownership and this condition continued when the Burlington was merged with its parent railroads to become the Burlington Northern, Inc. In 1982, the BN acquired the balance of the C&S stock and absorbed that road into its system as of the end of that year.

Another corporate change was the formation of Santa Fe Industries, Inc. which became the holding company of The Atchison, Topeka and Santa Fe Railway Company and its non-railroad affiliates effective August 21, 1968. There was no change in the management.

A similar revision was made in the SP corporate structure. On November 26, 1969, the Southern Pacific Company became a holding company and all of its railroads, and separately operated rail and trucking subsidiaries were transferred to a new company, the Southern Pacific Transportation Company. All of the stock of the latter company was held by the SP Company.

One of the most startling events occurred when the Southern Pacific and Santa Fe proposed a merger in May 1980. Extensive studies were made but, because certain issues could be resolved, negotiations were ended in October 1980.

The matter was revived in 1983 and, on December 23, 1983, Southern Pacific Company and Santa Fe Industries, Inc., the top holding companies, were merged as the Santa Fe Southern Pacific Corporation. (Commencing in May 1989, it became the Santa Fe Pacific Corporation.) An application was filed with the ICC to merge the underlying railroad systems. In the light of other recent rail mergers, many railroad men were much surprised in July 1986 when the ICC denied the application. So, the Southern Pacific Transportation Company continued as before to be operated independently under a trust. During the time the ICC was pondering its decision, a common red and yellow locomotive color scheme was adopted by both roads.

After the ICC denied a request for a reopening of the SP–Santa Fe merger application on June 30, 1987, the parent, SF-SP Corporation, decided to retain many but not all of the non-railroad assets as well as the Santa Fe Railway and sell the Southern Pacific Transportation Company and subsidiaries. Various groups submitted proposals for the acquisition of the SPTS, including Kansas City Southern Industries, Inc. and Rio Grande Industries, Inc., the parent of the Denver and Rio Grande Western Railroad. The Rio Grande application was approved by the ICC and the SPTS and affiliates became a wholly owned subsidiary of the Rio Grande on October 13, 1988. The two railroads, while coordinating their activities, are operated separately at this time.

New Mexico is fortunate to have two non-profit groups interpreting the history of New Mexico railroads.

The Friends of the Cumbres and Toltec Scenic Railroad is a "hands-on" restoration group whose goals include the restoration and display of historic equipment and structures and the operation of a volunteer program. The Friends publishes a newsletter, the *C&TS Dispatch*, which includes articles on matters pertaining to this historic property. Membership can be obtained by a $15.00 tax-deductible donation sent to the Friends at P.O. Box 222, Chama, New Mexico, 87520.

The Railroad Club of New Mexico publishes a bi-monthly newsletter about various New Mexico railroad topics and also holds bi-monthly meetings, normally in Albuquerque. Annual dues are $10.00 and membership can be obtained by sending the dues to Railroad Club of New Mexico, P.O. Box 36052, Station D, Albuquerque, New Mexico, 87176.

"Men against the Mountains" is a title suggested by this struggle. *Heading northward to Raton Pass, this train is near Lynn, New Mexico, and will soon enter the tunnel. Built by Baldwin in 1923, these 2-10-2s are numbered 3874 and, by coincidence, 3873. Santa Fe Railway.*

THE ATCHISON, TOPEKA
AND SANTA FE RAILWAY

Santa Fe

The year was 1859, the place was Topeka, Kansas, and the legislature made history by granting a charter to the group headed by Cyrus Holliday endeavoring to form the Atchison and Topeka Railroad Company. Four years went by with little accomplished other than talk, planning and a change of name to the more ambitious Atchison, Topeka and Santa Fe Rail Road Company. Stretching out the route seemed to lengthen the time before actual construction began but, finally and again in Topeka, work commenced on a fall day in 1868. The first segment was opened the following year but the good people of Atchison had to wait several years for the Santa Fe trains, for now the rails from Topeka were headed only to the west. Moving on, the Santa Fe took advantage of prosperous times and was at Dodge City in 1872 to help that town take its place in western folklore as a cattle shipping point. Four years later Holliday's tracks reached Pueblo, Colorado, and building southwesterly from La Junta, another Santa Fe line (the Pueblo and Arkansas Valley R. R.)

was completed to Trinidad, in Southern Colorado, near the end of the summer of 1878. Located on the north side of the Raton Mountains, the gateway into the Territory of New Mexico, Trinidad was the key point for the railroad assault on Raton Pass. Here was to take place one of the classic railroad races for a pass, probably the first such encounter by rival factions in the Far West.

Watching Raton Pass with equal interest was that remarkable railroad of a large dimension, the Denver and Rio Grande Railway Company. "Large dimension" refers to its total projected length of some 2,400 miles from Denver to Mexico City and not to its width. Though its rails were only 36 inches apart, it was a narrow-gauge railway in the grandest manner, as the several histories of that line establish in detail.

Heading the Denver and Rio Grande was General William J. Palmer who had constructed several railroads and surveyed others, including the Kansas Pacific extension into New Mexico and Arizona, a projected line which never materialized. On the other hand, Palmer's Rio Grande was a most viable railroad, marching down along the abrupt east face of the Rockies from Denver to Colorado Springs and Pueblo in 1871–72. Four years later the road's mileage was augmented by another 86 miles almost reaching the New Mexico boundary, terminating at El Moro, a new townsite laid out by Palmer four miles east of Trinidad, the county seat of Las Animas County. The citizens of Trinidad were less than pleased with this move and, to make matters worse, Palmer continued his railroad south for another seven miles to Engleville the following year (1877).

Raton Pass was the scene of much activity even before the rival railroads made preliminary surveys. Some years earlier, "Uncle Dick" Wootton had graded a wagon road over the pass, established a hotel and collected tolls for use of his road. Although both railroads had made surveys, neither the Santa Fe nor the Rio Grande had taken the necessary step of filing their locations with the Department of the Interior, so that the pass was left "open," awaiting the first claimant.

Even before the Santa Fe built to Trinidad, it had made careful plans to gain control of Raton Pass. The report of construction for 1878, signed by William B. Strong, Vice President and General Manager of the Santa Fe and later its president,

The station at Raton, built around 1910, utilized some interesting architecture. John E. Southwell Collection.

The Raton tunnels are in New Mexico, just across the Colorado boundary. The first Raton tunnel was opened in 1879 to replace a temporary switch-back. A second, lower bore was completed in 1908 (right) and was used for west-bound trains. With the advent of T.C.S. (C.T.C.), the original tunnel was abandoned in 1949. The rails of the second main track were removed from the summit to the city of Raton, and all trains used the newer tunnel. Santa Fe Railway.

in the stockholders' report for that year, summarized the event as follows:

"It having been determined to extend the Pueblo and Arkansas Valley Railroad from La Junta to the boundary line of Colorado and New Mexico, to connect with a road to be constructed in a south-westerly direction by a company called the New Mexico and Southern Pacific Railroad Company, organized in our interest, the necessary preparations were made; and on the 26th February 1878 we took possession of Raton Pass, the only practicable route for a railroad over the Raton Mountains and commenced the work of construction. Our possession was disputed for a time by the Denver and Rio Grande Railway Company but later that commpany retired from the contest, and work on the new line has steadily progressed."

Strong's simplified version of the hassle if somewhat amplified would reveal that when two top Santa Fe construction men, A. A. Robinson and William R. Morley, spotted two key engineers in the employ of General Palmer heading for Trinidad early in 1878, they realized that they had better act and act fast. One night, just before Uncle Dick Wootton was about to turn in, Robinson and Morley called on him to discuss their desired purpose, stressing urgency in the matter. Men were rounded up in the middle of the night, handed shovels and sent to the top of the pass to join Louis Kingman, a Santa Fe advance surveyor, in starting the grade for the railroad. As the first to initiate construction, the Santa Fe's prior right to the pass was established and, once that was done, the Santa Fe men could temporarily retire from the scene. Early the next morning, Morley and Robinson realized how close the race had been, for at the bottom of the pass a Rio Grande grading crew had been assembled ready to go to work. (Though that conflict was resolved, the Santa Fe–Rio Grande battles were not over, for in April, only a few months after this incident, they were battling in the Royal Gorge, some 40 miles west of Pueblo, Colorado.)

Once the right to the pass had been secured, the next job was to build the grade and drill the tunnel through its summit. The tunnel, requiring more time to complete than had been contemplated, was temporarily by-passed by a series of switchbacks and, on December 7, 1878, the first car passed into New Mexico at a point 15.7 miles south of Trinidad. At the head

The Depot Hotel at Las Vegas drew a large crowd to witness the departure of the decorated funeral train of former Governor M. A. Otero.

end was "Uncle Avery" Turner and to him belongs the honor of piloting the first steam train into New Mexico.

Now that Santa Fe forces were in New Mexico, they pushed south and westerly, passing Willow Springs (later Raton), then crossing the highlands east of the Sangre de Cristo Mountains through Springer and Wagon Mound to reach Las Vegas by July 4, 1879. Two months later trains began using the Raton Tunnel and the Santa Fe paid its first dividend.

Beyond lay Santa Fe, the first major goal of the railroad, but to reach that important city, there was a problem of several grades. Working their way between piñon pine and juniper-covered mesas, the surveyors found a way to Santa Fe, following streams and rivers where practicable. For many miles the route continued in a canyon carved by the upper part of the Pecos River, then along the usually dry Glorieta Creek to the pass of the same name. At that summit the railroad entered the watershed of the Rio Grande, as the tracks went down the

Santa Fe station architecture is an interesting example of adaptation to local tradition and culture. The Wagon Mound depot (top), typical of Santa Fe stations across Missouri, Kansas, and eastern New Mexico, is 1898 Railroad Standard, and virtually identical specimens can be found on the Katy, Rock Island, or a dozen granger roads. The little Santa Fe depot, however, is a pleasing example of mission-style architecture, even to the tile roof, that blends well with the Spanish heritage of the Rio Grande country. The Las Vegas depot and Casteñada Hotel present more of an architectural compromise.

At Ribera, the Santa Fe crosses the upper part of the Pecos River and, in the intervening five miles east to Blanchard station, the grade includes interesting curves, to the delight of photographers. In October 1947, Richard Kindig photographed a section of the westbound California Limited *working across New Mexico behind 4-8-4 locomotives. The third section, with No. 3779, snakes around an* **S***-curve near Blanchard, having just passed over the other part of the curve moments earlier. Note the grade visible over the sleeping cars.* **R. H. Kindig photograph.**

narrow canyon of Galisteo Creek (where eastbound grades of 3% still prevail) to Galisteo Junction, later renamed Lamy to honor a prominent bishop. At Galisteo Junction, the course abruptly turned north to Santa Fe. The first train arrived in the Territorial Capital on February 9, 1880 to be properly welcomed by flowing speeches and a parade.

Impossible mountain ranges precluded the location of Santa Fe on the main line; reluctantly the engineers relegated the capital to branch line status and continued the main line west and south from Galisteo Junction to Bernalillo, where it met the Rio Grande. Flowing southward, this river provided an easy gradient all the way to Rincon and El Paso. Albuquerque was reached on April 10, 1880. A few days after that, a special train brought down several hundred people from the capital to help celebrate the event and soon Pullman sleeping cars served the new terminus.

A Baldwin 2-8-0 paused at Glorieta in 1880. Glorieta was the summit dividing the Pecos River and Rio Grande watersheds. **Museum of New Mexico..**

The name of the affiliate of the Santa Fe, The New Mexico and Southern Pacific Railroad, was indicative of its objective. The Southern Pacific, building eastward from California, had crossed the Colorado River to enter Arizona at Yuma on September 30, 1877 and was pushing across that territory. In March 1880, just a month after the Santa Fe arrived at New Mexico's capital, the SP's rails were in Tucson and by the end of the year its tracks were well inside the border of New Mexico with El Paso, Texas, not very far away.

The Santa Fe contractors were following the engineers' stakes along the Rio Grande during the summer and fall of 1880. By the middle of July, the railroad was making regular freight deliveries in Socorro, an old Spanish town with a mission dating back to 1598, and now taking on added importance as the center of a mining area. Progress was made but it was not always easy going. Washouts caused by the typical summer storms of the southwest tied up parts of the line for a week, slowing down to a trickle the flow of necessary supplies.

In 1896, the ticket office at Albuquerque was between the signs reading "Ladies Waiting Room" and "Gents Waiting Room." Museum of New Mexico.

A quiet moment in the Albuquerque yard in 1880. James S. Wroth Collection.

The local train between Belen and Albuquerque late in a fall afternoon. R. H. Kindig photograph.

The corporate name of the Santa Fe affiliate building in New Mexico was the New Mexico and Southern Pacific Railroad Company, which held title to 372 miles in the territory. The lettering on the tender, though faint, designates this ownership, and the locomotive, No. 47, bore the name "Del Norte." The location of this train and the circumstances relating to the combination of this well-dressed man, his wife, and her dog are a mystery. Colorado Railroad Museum Collection.

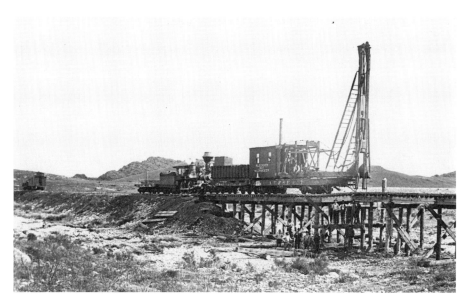

The locomotive is unidentified, but the lettering on the cab of the pile driver reads "Pile Driver, No. 7, Rio Grande Div." Trestle repairs were a frequent occurrence in the Southwest. Colorado Railroad Museum Collection.

By the end of November 1880, the Santa Fe could point with pride to a railroad extending all the way from Atchison, Kansas, to San Marcial, New Mexico, a span of over 1,000 miles. Rails had been spiked down for another 39 miles to Martin's Wells but that part was not yet in operation. A new corporation was formed to carry on the work south of San Marcial, the Rio Grande, Mexico and Pacific Railroad; but, again, it was affiliated with the Santa Fe.

The southern transcontinental railroad route was soon to be a reality and was welcomed not only for its convenience in distant travel but also because of its expected civilizing influence in the territory. Some travelers were not willing to wait for the gap between the Southern Pacific and the Santa Fe to be closed; in November 1880 people were using the regular stage from Rio Mimbres (near Deming) to San Marcial, initially paying $20.00 for the 120 mile trip.

Even the coming of the railroads failed to halt violence and murder. Though Victorio and his band of Apache Indians were

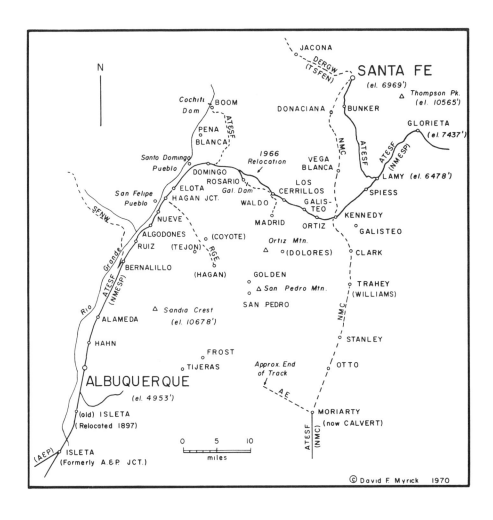

© David F. Myrick 1970

now quiet, a stage was attacked almost within sight of Deming and its occupants slaughtered. A local feud ended in the death of a newspaper editor in Socorro just after Christmas 1880 and a few days later the corpse of a Santa Fe contractor was found at Doña Ana (near Mesilla), pierced by four bullets.

At Rincon, 75 miles south of San Marcial, the line split with one section going to Deming and the other to El Paso, Texas. With the driving of a silver spike at Deming in the afternoon of March 8, 1881 before a small handful of railroad people and a few newspaper men, the Southern Pacific and the Santa Fe were joined and the second transcontinental railroad was born. The first through train left Kansas City for Deming on March

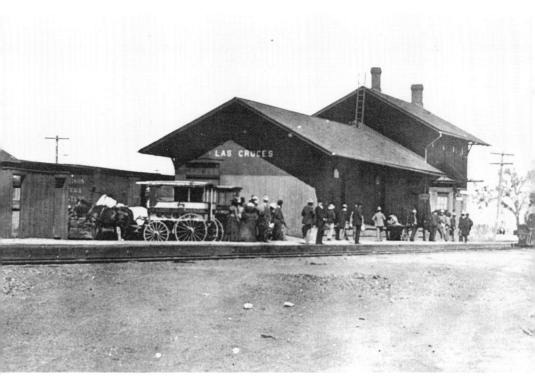

A crowd awaits the arrival of the train at Las Cruces in the lower Rio Grande Valley. **Santa Fe Railway.**

17 with seven cars, said to be "all crowded."

While the Santa Fe had completed 550 miles of railroad in New Mexico in slightly more than two years, Deming was merely a stepping stone in the plans to reach the Pacific Coast. Interests friendly to the Santa Fe had begun building the Sonora Railway northward from the magnificent harbor of Guaymas on the Gulf of California and after some delays, because the location of the route had not been resolved with the Mexican government, the railway was able to make good progress. By using the SP's tracks from Deming to Benson, Arizona, and then building the New Mexico and Arizona Railroad to Nogales on the Mexican border, the Santa Fe achieved a line from Kansas City to the Pacific Coast when the last spike was driven at Nogales on October 25, 1882. (El Paso greeted its second railroad on June 11, 1881 when the Santa Fe completed 20 miles of railroad in

All the lines forming the Santa Fe Route between Kansas City and California were included in this elaborate lettered timetable. The cover of the May 1885 issue, less than two years after the opening of the line, was printed with brown ink on a light orange background.

Tourists from the East bound for California were fascinated by the life-style of the Indians. From the windows of the passing cars, the travelers had a close view of the Laguna Indian Pueblo, 69 miles west of Albuquerque. **Santa Fe Railway.**

Texas under the name of Rio Grande & El Paso Railroad which, with a change of name in 1914, became the Rio Grande, El Paso and Santa Fe Railroad.)

Though Santa Fe construction initially ended in New Mexico at Deming in March 1881, through other corporate entities construction was carried on for many years. Five branches in New Mexico (Hot Springs, Carthage, Blossburg, Lake Valley and Magdalena) were built by The New Mexican Railroad Company from 1882 to 1884. More important lines follow in this chapter while other branches are covered in the chapters relating to coal, lumber, mining and street cars.

Just three years after the Santa Fe rails joined the Southern Pacific at Deming, its public timetables called attention to the "Three Lines to the Pacific Coast." "Number One is the Great

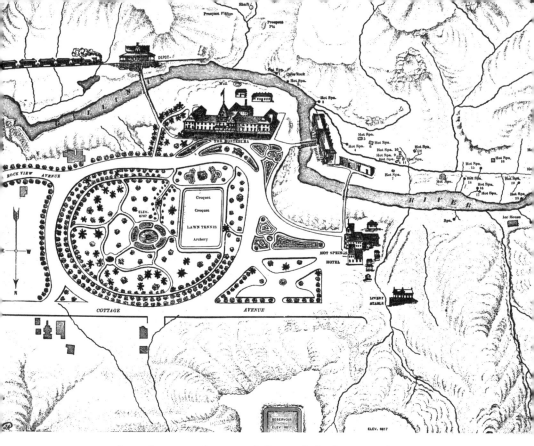

A tourist promotion map delineated the location of The Montezuma Hotel *and related facilities in the late nineteenth century.* Museum of New Mexico Collection.

Needles Route" via Albuquerque, A&P to The Needles and SP Railroad to San Francisco. "Number Two is the Los Angeles Route" via Deming and the SPRR to San Francisco. "Number Three runs through Salt Lake City and Ogden," the traveler was told, via Pueblo, D&RG to Ogden and the Central Pacific to San Francisco.

Also extolled in this same folder were the virtues of the Santa Fe Route to the City of Mexico via El Paso and the Mexican Central Railway. It offered "12 Hours Shorter Time" than any other line from Kansas City, Chicago or New York.

Frequent references in the folder were made to places in New Mexico, such as Santa Fe and the Montezuma Hotel at the Hot Springs near Las Vegas. Though it had burned January

17, 1884, a new fireproof structure was rising and the Santa Fe cast all modesty aside when it declared that it would be "the most palatial inn between Chicago and San Francisco."

Atlantic and Pacific Railroad

Although the Santa Fe had an all-rail route to California with the Southern Pacific interchange at Deming and had its own rail and sea route to California through Guaymas, it lacked a short, direct line to the Pacific Coast and particularly to Southern California. Hopefully some better way to the Coast could be found and fortunately for the Boston men running the Santa Fe, just such an opportunity presented itself.

It all began with an effort which culminated in an Act of Congress approved July 27, 1866 forming the Atlantic and Pacific Railroad Company. The authorized route was from Springfield, Missouri, to the Canadian River, to Albuquerque then via Agua Fria "or other suitable pass" to the headwaters of the Little Colorado River and along the 35th parallel to the Pacific. A branch line from Van Buren, Arkansas to the Canadian River was also approved in the act.

There was a land grant and a list of distinguished sponsors to further the cause, but progress in 1873 consisted of only 327 unimpressive miles in Missouri and Eastern Oklahoma. More important, the company was in the hands of a receiver. Reorganization and a new name, St. Louis and San Francisco Railway, followed, but the basic question of "how do we get the cash to build" still persisted. It was at this critical time that the Santa Fe men entered the picture, with discussions beginning in 1879 that led to the "Tripartite Agreement" of January 31, 1880. By this agreement, the AT&SF shared the ownership of the stock of the Atlantic and Pacific with the SL&SF and the two parents agreed to undertake the financing and building of the Western Division of the A&P from A&P Junction (near Albuquerque) toward the Pacific Coast.

A celebration was held in Albuquerque on April 8, 1880 with civic leaders on hand to mark the beginning of the construction of the Western Division of the A&P. Though the turn-off point to the west was at A&P Junction (Isleta), 15 miles

The contrast between the diminutive switcher, A&P No. 2 (0-6-0), standing by No. 19 (New Mexico), a road locomotive built by the Rhode Island Works, is apparent in this photograph from 1880. James S. Wroth Collection.

south of Albuquerque, operations of the A&P began at the latter place, the 15 miles involving the use of some of its own tracks but mostly NM&SP (AT&SF) trackage.

To forestall troublesome encroachment from rival railroad men, some gangs of graders were promptly dispatched to initiate work at distant points, one as far away as Querino Cañon (Rio Puerco) in Arizona. Instead of rivals, it was troublesome Navajos that sent advance grading forces scurrying to seek cover.

The first rails were spiked down in July 1880 and 25 miles of grade were reported to be complete early in August. At that time there were 35 miles of rails in the Albuquerque yards ready to move west to the front while another 100 miles of track and fittings were on the road from St. Louis. The tracks soon passed through the Laguna Pueblo and the Indians there, who had found it entertaining to pull up Louis Kingman's survey stakes, were now hopping on a morning freight train to return the same evening with a good load of fire wood.

An early schedule called for a 7:00 AM departure from Albuquerque, a lunch stop at Cubero and arrival at Fulton at 12:55

The San Francisco Chief *offered rail travelers luxury accommo-*
dations as it sped across New Mexico. This point is about twenty
miles west of Grants. **Santa Fe Railway.**

PM. (Fulton, a short-lived name, was just a few miles west of McCarty's.) Campbell's Pass (Continental Divide—el. 7,248') was crossed by the steam cars in March 1881, an event one scribe likened to the crossing of the Rubicon. In the late spring of 1881, track layers were beyond the New Mexico line, pushing their way across Arizona and after two more years of work, matching wits against frustrating delays, the builders had crossed Arizona. The Southern Pacific Railroad had built across the desert from Mojave to Needles, California, and on August 9, 1883, with the driving of the last spike at the Colorado River bridge, the "Thirty-fifth Parallel Trans-Continental Line" was finished and ready for business.

The construction of the railroad gave birth to short-lived, "hell on wheels" towns which moved westward along with "The Front." Some towns were of more permanent nature and are important cities of today. Coolidge, just beyond the Continental Divide and 136 miles from Albuquerque, was named for T. Jefferson Coolidge, president of the Santa Fe during this construction. Grants was named for the Grant brothers, contractors who built many miles of railroads in the west. Gallup, which took its name from an A&P paymaster, became a division terminal in lieu of Coolidge in 1889 because of its close proximity to the coal mines.

The "Gay Nineties" may have earned that name for the life and times of some individuals but the depression of 1893 was anything but joyous for it adversely affected individuals and corporations without respect for position. Many corporations fell on hard times; the Santa Fe, the Frisco and their offspring, the A&P, found themselves in the hands of receivers. In the reorganizations that followed, the Santa Fe acquired full ownership of the former Western Division of the A&P in 1897 through the subsidiary Santa Fe Pacific Railroad, until 1902 when the railroad property was absorbed by the parent company. Through a series of steps spread over the years, the Santa Fe also obtained ownership of the former SP Mojave–Needles line in California.

Belen Cutoff

Though the Santa Fe won the right to Raton Pass in 1878, it was not a complete victory from an operating standpoint, for the grades were a stubborn 3% or better thus necessitating double-headed trains. The best way to avoid these grades was to build around them and that is what was done by employing a long-contemplated route through Eastern New Mexico and the Texas Panhandle to meet the main lines in Kansas.

With the acquisition of the railroad in Pecos Valley and the subsequent extension to Amarillo, Texas, where it joined other tracks of the Santa Fe, a large portion of the second route was already realized. Remaining was a gap of some 200 miles between a point near the Texas–New Mexico boundary and Belen, 30 miles south of Albuquerque on the line to El Paso.

Around 1900–1902 various railroads were engaged in active construction in New Mexico with Albuquerque as one of their possible objectives, the Rock Island and the Santa Fe Central being examples. The most convenient crossing of the mountain range east of the Rio Grande, from the position of the AT&SF, was at Abo Pass, about 25 miles southeast of Belen, which in

Part of the construction necessitated by the Belen Cutoff in 1907 was a bridge over Abo River near Sais on the west side of the pass. **Santa Fe Railway.**

turn is 30 miles south of Albuquerque. To avoid possible legal or physical conflict with other interested parties, they decided that the time to initiate work was now at hand. Accordingly, surveys were begun and a Santa Fe subsidiary, The Eastern Railway Company of New Mexico, was incorporated October 30, 1902.

Early in 1903 a construction contract was awarded to B. Lantry & Son, a well known construction firm with headquarters in Strong City, Kansas. Almost at once a large force of men was dispatched to begin work at Abo Pass, the most strategic point and the location of the most difficult work on the new line.

Belen soon became a lively spot. By the end of January 1903, tracks were laid almost to the Rio Grande and a temporary pile bridge was soon thrown across the river to facilitate the movement of supplies to the graders' camps, the most important being at Abo Pass where the rock work and grading were being "pushed." To supply the wants of the workers, 75 freight teams were constantly on the road from Belen to the five camps. At Belen, the limited sleeping accommodations were soon exhausted. Even the floor of the railroad station was requisitioned every night by snoring, blanketed figures while, along the grade, numerous campfires were surrounded by men seeking work.

The money markets of the nation began tightening during the year to culminate in the "Rich Man's Panic." The Rock Island suspended work on their Tucumcari-Amarillo connection and the Santa Fe, to conserve funds for other construction, halted work on the Belen Cutoff. In July 1903, when work ceased, some 20 miles of rail had been laid east from Belen and much of the grading up the arroyo to the summit had been accomplished. As the eastern portion of this line had not been definitely located, surveyors were still at work around Tucumcari.

Local residents expected work to be resumed in 1904 but they were a little ahead of the schedule for tools were not taken up again until August 1905. Though contractors faced difficulties in obtaining laborers and finding water, the grade continued to stretch out. In January 1906 there were 300 men at work on the western end, with others on the east end, and it was planned to expand the forces considerably when the weather became warmer. In total, the project as completed involved 278 miles of which 249 were between Belen and Texico.

Nestled by the tracks were the new towns which sprang up with the coming of the railroad. One was Sunnyside, 69 miles west of Texico, to which the Eastern Railway was completed in the early part of March 1906. "Sunnyside on the Pecos is a great town" . . . was the way one description began in September 1905. It went on to say that Sunnyside then had seven saloons, three restaurants and some tents. There was hope that there might be some truth in the rumor that the new cluster would be a division point and some forward-looking citizens were putting up shacks. Though Vaughn became the division point because of its location, Sunnyside continued to grow but under the name of Fort Sumner.

AT&SF No. 3311, with a 2-6-6-2 wheel arrangement, was one of the 24 Mallets built by Baldwin in 1911. Mountainair, with an elevation of 6,492 feet (as it looked about 1917), is at the high point on the Belen Cutoff. H. J. Maxwell Collection.

A few weeks after the railroad was opened to Sunnyside, the western segment of 109 miles from Belen to the crossing of the El Paso and Rock Island was completed. The actual crossing of the EP&RI was made by long fills and an overpass with the station of Vaughn at the east end. Three miles west of Vaughn on the EP&RI was Epris (called Llano prior to 1905) with a multitude of houses of refreshment. These saloons were such a deterrent to construction that a court injunction was secured to close them.

Even though the line was not fully completed, commercial trains operated over the new tracks when the first timetable went into effect on December 18, 1907. At that time the depression of 1907 was under way and work was temporarily sus-

A long string of refrigerator cars crossed Abo Pass near Moun-
tainair with No. 5022, a 2-10-4 type, on the point. Built by Baldwin
in 1944, this was in the lot of 25 locomotives which constituted
the Santa Fe's final purchase of new steam locomotives. **Santa Fe**
Railway.

pended in February 1908 so that when it was turned over to
the operating department on July 1, 1908, there was much
fencing and ballasting still to be accomplished.

As part of the through line, there were changes made at
each end. West from Belen, a 19-mile connection was built to
Dalies and Rio Puerco and, with the completion of the alternate
link from Sandia to Dalies, a part of the original A&P (Sandia
to Rio Puerco) was abandoned in 1908. At the eastern end, the
northern part of the Pecos Valley branch was moved from Texico nine miles west to Clovis where a large division point was
established with important shops and a roundhouse.

Built to avoid heavy grades, the new line accomplished its
purpose admirably. The heaviest grade was the $1\frac{1}{4}$% climb
from Belen to Abo Pass (westbound was only $\frac{6}{10}$ of 1%). Some
time went by before transcontinental passenger trains were

Mechanization of the railroad industry contributed to its economic survival. While moving along one rail, the adzers make a seat for tie plates in preparation for the installation of new 132-pound rail near Fort Sumner, 60 miles west of Clovis. **Santa Fe Railway.**

using the Belen Cutoff (also called Santa Fe Cutoff during construction). Early trains included *The Scout* and *The Missionary* while later schedules list the *San Francisco Chief.* Freight traffic from California to Chicago as well as Texas continued to grow enough to warrant short sections of double track between Vaughn and Clovis. In 1943–44, centralized traffic control was installed and in 1944 the roundhouses at Clovis and Belen were extended to accommodate larger locomotives.

Colmor Cutoff

Maps in the Santa Fe timetables for many years before World War II carried a dotted line in Northeastern New Mexico symbolizing "lines under construction" and later, as the years went

Construction of the Colmor Cutoff in northern New Mexico was a long-held dream of Santa Fe officials to shorten the main line. When the grading was done in the summer of 1931, the contractors used tractors instead of mules to form the grade. The scene is five miles east of Clayton. Santa Fe Railway.

by, "lines projected." Though a short cut around Raton Pass and a Santa Fe line linking Colorado and Texas had been in the formative stage for many years, it was not until 1930 that the Santa Fe sought authority from the ICC for their construction. Among the lines approved by the ICC was the Colmor Cutoff.

The Santa Fe had built a 120-mile line from Dodge City to Elkhart, Kansas, in 1913 which, under the name of the Elkhart & Santa Fe Railway, was extended another 59 miles into Oklahoma in 1925, passing through Boise City and terminating at Felt. Under the same corporate name, it was proposed to build the Colmor Cutoff from Felt for another 110 miles, crossing the Colorado and Southern at Clayton, New Mexico, and continuing west to join the Santa Fe main line at Colmor, an old railroad station 11 miles south of Springer and 60 miles north of Las Vegas, New Mexico.

When Santa Fe rails reached Farley, 35 miles southwest of Mount Dora, all work on the Colmor Cutoff ceased. Here the Santa Fe built a Standard No. 3 Depot, a coal house, and a five-room agent's house nearby. The time is late November 1931, and already some winter snow has fallen. Santa Fe Railway.

The advantages of this shortcut were obvious. Not only would the transcontinental route be shortened by 69 miles but Raton Pass with its grades of better than 3% would be circumvented. Additionally, it was expected that new traffic from livestock and increased plantings of winter wheat would be developed by this line.

Work commenced shortly after receiving ICC approval in the spring of 1930 but long before graders approached Clayton an agreement was reached with the C&S for joint use of 17 miles of their line to Mt. Dora, thus avoiding the duplication of trackage and reducing the cost of the $6.5 million Santa Fe line by a half million dollars. After reaching Clayton and jumping to Mt. Dora, construction continued westerly for 35.6 miles to Farley, where regular train service began November 15, 1931. Work on the remaining 35 miles to Colmor was deferred until economic conditions improved.

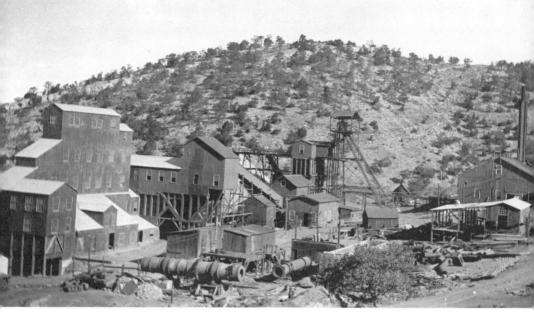

West of Socorro, a 27-mile branch served the mining town of Mag-dalena. U.S. Geological Survey.

Conditions did improve and the Santa Fe resumed construction on the other lines but not on the Colmor Cutoff. Operated as the Clayton District of the New Mexico Division, a mixed train, originating at Boise City, made the daily round trip. Twice a week in the early 1930s the train went all the way to Farley (95.5 miles) but by 1940 the operation had been reduced to one solitary trip each week.

During World War II, the War Production Board, seeking badly needed scrap metal, was scouting for little used rail lines. This branch was considered a likely candidate. Not only did little traffic originate on this line, its importance as a part of a future transcontinental line had diminished. Considerable improvements had been made to both the La Junta route and the Belen Cutoff thus speeding train movements. For fast freight service, the Belen Cutoff with its modest grades would have largely offset the combination of heavy grades over Glorieta Pass and the shorter mileage. After hearings, the ICC authorized the abandonment from Boise City to Farley and operations ceased in 1942.

The only station along the way was Water Canyon where mixed trains stopped on flag in 1940. **Fred Springer photograph.**

There is little today at Mt. Dora. A livestock corral and a former section house along the C&S and a ranch house about make up the town. The most prominent feature, unused and neglected for almost half a century, is the long grade leading toward Farley.

Santa Fe Lines in New Mexico

Part of the original line of the Santa Fe to the Pacific Coast incorporated the easy grade along the Rio Grande. This could be a blessing or a terror depending on the river's mood, which varied with the seasons. This segment of the railroad, affectionately known as the "Horny Toad" Division because of the abundance of the little desert creatures, felt the full effect of rampages of the Rio Grande. For example, during the months from May to October 1884, the Rio Grande abandoned its old channel in many places to attack the track so that for five months it was a constant struggle to keep the trains running.

Not too many years ago, the Kaiser Steel plant was flourishing at Fontana, California, just east of Los Angeles. Coal for the furnaces came from York Canyon in unit trains. With Cerro Colorado in the background, five 900-class SD-24 units are moving 84,000 tons of coal and have just passed Lamy. **Santa Fe Railway.**

The branch to El Paso was entirely closed for two months and north of Rincon over six miles of railroad had to be relocated.

Though 1884 was a busy year along this line, things had quieted enough to permit the construction of the branch from Socorro to Magdalena near the close of the year. Known primarily as a lead-zinc mining district, Magdalena was also an important livestock shipping point. A two-mile spur from Magdalena tapped the mines at Kelly; some ores were treated there while other ore was sent to the smelter at Socorro. Declining traffic brought an end to the 26-mile Magdalena branch, which was abandoned on November 20, 1972.

Maps of New Mexico in the few years prior to World War I sometimes indicate a branch from Butte Junction (near Engle) to the Elephant Butte Dam, nine miles to the west. The dam was part of an irrigation project, utilizing the waters of the Rio Grande, and was completed in 1916. Built in 1904 to bring in construction materials, the branch was abandoned in 1917, having completed its purpose. Because of its location south of San Marcial, the dam was no help in preventing the two floods in 1929 which wiped out the town, once an important stop on the way to El Paso.

Stories of the men and machines that made the Santa Fe an institution in New Mexico can be told by the hundreds and some have already found their way to the printed page. Space limitations preclude mentioning them here but some of the traditional trains should not escape notice.

Until the Golden State Route via El Paso was opened in 1902, the Santa Fe had the only short line from Chicago to Los Angeles. During 1907, three pairs of transcontinental trains operated through New Mexico but, in the late 1920s the number had doubled. The Santa Fe was solicitous of its travelers and famous steam trains, such as *The Chief, California Limited* and *Grand Canyon Limited* were usually scheduled to pause in Albuquerque for thirty minutes enabling passengers to visit the Indian shops adjoining the station. It also allowed train servicing as Albuquerque had some of the most extensive shops on the system.

In the 1930s, changes began to take place in passenger trains as the railroads entered the streamline era. The *Super Chief* was the first name train on the Santa Fe to be powered by a

Inaugurated in 1926, The Chief *was Santa Fe's premier train for ten years until the advent of the streamliners. With two helpers added at Raton, the eastbound* Chief *is near Keota on its way to the Raton tunnel. It was a time of transition between heavy-weight and light-weight equipment.* **Santa Fe Railway.**

diesel (a flat-nosed model built in 1935 gave way to the stream-lined locomotive of silver, yellow and red in 1937). The stream-lined *Super Chief* and *El Capitan* trains began making trips in 1938. In freight service, the end of the steam age had its first indication in February 1941 when a demonstration run of a General Motors–Electro-motive Division 5400 HP locomotive ran from Chicago to Los Angeles, stopping at major terminals along the way for public inspection. At Amarillo and Gallup, crowds swarmed about the new style of motive power. Within two decades there was a complete change as repair shops were converted to diesel servicing or vanished entirely along with steam locomotives and the tall water towers.

Notwithstanding the rising auto and airline competition, the number of main-line trains on the Santa Fe in 1946 equaled the number operated in 1929 but the number of extra sections in the later years was but a shadow of former times. By 1970, the Santa Fe operated only three transcontinental trains: the combined *Super Chief* and *El Capitan* and Nos. 23 and 24, the former *Grand Canyon Limited* which, except for a small part of its route, no longer carried sleeping cars. These trains climbed over Raton Pass while the *San Francisco Chief* was operated via Amarillo and entered the state near Clovis.

When Amtrak took over Santa Fe passenger service on May 1, 1971, the number of transcontinental trains were slimmed down from three to a single train, *Super Chief–El Capitan*, Nos. 17 and 18. Soon the name was changed to the *Southwest Limited* but, after the introduction of Superliners cars, the train became the *Southwest Chief* in April 1985.

No record of the Santa Fe in New Mexico should be written without a brief nod to its contribution to the tourist industry of the state which was done in conjunction with the ubiquitous Fred Harvey and his magic spell. Of English birth, Fred Harvey decided to do something about the atrocious meal stops along railroads where no dining car service was provided. Going into sort of a partnership with the Santa Fe, his restaurants soon stretched along the whole system, his "Harvey Girls" undoubtedly contributing to the "taming of the West." Besides railroad eating stations, Fred Harvey operated dining rooms and hotels. Of the latter, there were eight in New Mexico, The Alvarado of Albuquerque with 119 rooms being the largest and the four-room hotel at Vaughn the smallest. Most famous of the hotels in New Mexico is La Fonda in Santa Fe.

Fred Harvey service extended into the dining cars on Santa Fe trains and to tours of the southwestern United States. Well known were the Indian Detours, started in 1926, which offered two and three day side trips. Fred Harvey buses met passengers stepping off the train at Lamy, whisked them to La Fonda and then guided them to such pueblos as Puyé and Taos with a courier in each bus. One of the claims was that their buses would return passengers to connecting trains on time, not always an easy accomplishment before modern highways. Summer cloudbursts washed out roads and bridges, almost as part

At Arriba, a station just three miles north of Las Vegas, the cameraman climbed a signal tower to capture the two Chiefs meeting at a siding almost mid-way between Chicago and Los Angeles. Santa Fe Railway.

it's fun to travel

Santa Fe

SUPER CHIEF—Trains 17 and 18
Daily, Chicago—Kansas City—Los Angeles
All Private Room Sleeping Car Service

Dormitory Car . . . Chicago—Los Angeles.
Turquoise Room (for private dining) and Pleasure Dome Lounge Car . . . Chicago—Los Angeles.
Dining Car . . . Chicago—Los Angeles.
Sleeping Cars . . Chicago—Los Angeles.
Roomettes, Bedrooms and Suites.
Radio and recorded musical programs in all cars, stock reports, newspapers and periodicals, "wake-up" coffee and other deluxe service.
Courier Nurse Service.

EL CAPITAN—Trains 17 and 18
Daily, Chicago—Kansas City—Los Angeles
All-Chair-Car Service
All seats reserved.

Baggage Car . . Chicago—Los Angeles.
Dormitory—Baggage Car . . . Chicago—Los Angeles.
Hi-Level Lounge Car . . Chicago—Los Angeles.
Observation deck and refreshments on upper level.
Kachina Coffee Shop for Snacks on lower level.
Hi-Level Dining Car . . . Chicago—Los Angeles.
All seats on upper level.
Hi-Level Chair Cars . . . Chicago—Los Angeles.
Stretch-out, reclining seats with legrest, all reserved.
Radio and recorded music throughout train.
Courier Nurse Service.

Ask about the

One-price Ticket

No more ticket for this and ticket for that— pay for this and pay for that—when you use Santa Fe's One-Price Ticket.

It covers all your important travel costs while aboard Santa Fe trains, including rail transportation, chair or sleeping car accommodations, meals, even a pillow.

Now you can know in advance how little your Santa Fe trip will cost. Just ask about the One-Price Ticket plan for individual and family travel.

3

Westbound Condensed Transcontinental Passenger Schedules

Miles	Table 1	No. 23 See Note A Daily Example	No. 1 San Francisco Chief See Note A Daily Example	No. 17 Super Chief Extra Fare Daily Example	No. 17 El Capitan Extra Fare Daily Example
0	Chicago, Ill. (C.S.T.) Lv	9.00AM Sun.	10.00AM Sun.	6.30PM Sun.	6.30PM Sun.
38	Joliet Lv	9.55AM "	10.50AM "	7.20PM "	7.20PM "
58	Coal City Lv	B			
90	Streator Lv	10.45AM "	ⓐ11.35AM "	① 8.05PM "	① 8.05PM "
130	Chillicothe Lv	11.25AM "	12.10PM "	8.40PM "	8.40PM "
177	Galesburg, Ill. Lv	12.15PM "	12.55PM "	9.25PM "	9.25PM "
232	Ft. Madison, Iowa Lv	1.25PM "	2.00PM "	10.30PM Sun.	10.30PM Sun.
311	La Plata, Mo. Lv	2.58PM "	3.12PM "		
346	Marceline Lv	3.35PM "	3.50PM "		
385	Carrollton Lv	E 4.17PM "	4.25PM "		
449	Kansas City, Mo. Ar	5.40PM Sun.	5.50PM Sun.	1.55AM Mon.	1.55AM Mon.
	For complete schedule Kansas City-Tulsa, see Table 3, page 7.				
705	Tulsa, Okla. Ar	11.00PM Sun.	11.00PM Sun.		
449	Kansas City, Mo. Lv	6.00PM Sun.	6.20PM Sun.	2.05AM Mon.	2.05AM Mon.
489	Lawrence, Kan. Lv	6.40PM "	7.00PM "		
515	Topeka Lv	7.15PM "	7.35PM "		
550	Osage City Lv	ⓒ 7.50PM "			
577	Emporia Lv	C 8.30PM "	8.50PM "	ⓐ 3.55AM "	ⓐ 3.55AM "
650	Newton Ar	9.40PM "	9.50PM "	5.00AM "	5.00AM "
650	Newton Lv	9.45PM Sun.	10.05PM "	5.05AM Mon.	5.05AM Mon.
677	Wichita Lv		11.00PM "		
711	Wellington, Kan. Lv		11.45PM Sun.		
1023	Amarillo, Tex. Lv		5.30AM Mon.		
1126	Clovis, N.M. Lv		H 7.45AM Mon.		
668	Hutchinson, Kan. Lv	10.30PM Sun.	*For complete schedule Wichita-Belen, see Table 4, page 8.*	ⓐ 5.35AM Mon.	ⓐ 5.35AM Mon.
767	Kinsley (C.S.T.) Lv	11.58PM Mon.			
788	Dodge City (M.S.T.) Lv	12.10AM Mon.		6.18AM "	6.18AM "
838	Garden City Ar	D 1.05AM "		ⓑ 7.00AM "	ⓑ 7.00AM "
860	Lakin Lv	1.28AM "			
889	Syracuse, Kan. Ar	1.59AM "			
938	Lamar, Colo. Ar	2.46AM "		8.16AM "	8.16AM "
971	Las Animas Lv	3.16AM "			
990	La Junta, Colo. Ar	3.45AM Mon.		9.00AM Mon.	9.00AM Mon.
	For complete schedule La Junta-Denver, see Table 11, page 10.				
1172	Denver Ar	⊠ 8.40AM Mon.		⊠ 2.15PM Mon.	⊠ 2.15PM Mon.
1172	Denver Lv	⊠10.30PM Sun.			
990	La Junta Lv	E 4.00AM Mon.		9.20AM "	9.20AM "
1072	Trinidad, Colo. Lv	5.18AM "		10.37AM "	ⓐ10.37AM "
1094	Raton, N. M. Lv	L 6.18AM "		11.46AM "	11.46AM "
1204	Las Vegas Lv	8.08AM "		1.50PM "	1.50PM "
1268	Lamy Ar	9.50AM Mon.		3.40PM Mon.	3.40PM Mon.
1286	Santa Fe, N. M. Lv	ⓐ		ⓐ	ⓐ
1268	Lamy Lv	9.50AM Mon.		3.40PM "	3.40PM "
1319	Bernalillo Lv	E 10.37AM "			
1335	Albuquerque Ar	K 11.00AM "		5.00PM "	5.00PM "
1335	Albuquerque Lv	11.10AM Mon.		5.10PM "	5.10PM "
1367	Belen Ar		11.40AM Mon.		
1367	Belen Lv		11.59AM Mon.		
1406	Laguna Lv	ⓐ12.24PM Mon.			
1434	Grants Lv	12.54PM "			
1496	Gallup, N. M. Lv	K 2.05PM "	ⓐ1.21PM Mon.	7.38PM "	7.38PM "
1590	Holbrook, Ariz. Lv	3.23PM "	ⓐ3.36PM "		
1623	Winslow ◎ Lv	4.25PM "		9.35PM "	9.35PM "
1682	Flagstaff ◎ Lv	5.45PM Mon.	f 5.35PM Mon.	ⓐ10.45PM Mon.	ⓐ10.45PM Mon.
	For complete schedules Flagstaff-Grand Canyon and Flagstaff-Phoenix, see Table 6, page 8.				
1755	Grand Canyon ◎ Lv	⊠10.05AM Tues.	⊠10.05AM Tues.	⊠10.05AM Tues.	⊠10.05AM Tues.
1788	Phoenix ◎ Ar	⊠ 9.10PM Mon.	⊠ 9.10PM Mon.	⊠ 4.00AM Tues.	⊠ 4.00AM Tues.
	Grand Canyon ◎ Lv	⊠10.45AM Mon.	⊠10.45AM Mon.	7.00PM "	7.00PM "
	Phoenix ◎ Lv	⊠10.05AM Mon.	⊠10.05AM Mon.	⊠ 7.00PM Mon.	⊠ 7.00PM Mon.
1682	Flagstaff ◎ Lv	5.45PM Mon.	f 5.35PM Mon.	ⓐ10.45PM Mon.	ⓐ10.45PM Mon.
1765	Seligman ◎ Lv	K 7.30PM "	7.20PM "	12.32AM Tues.	12.32AM Tues.
1853	Kingman, Ariz. (M.S.T.) ◎ Lv	8.58PM "	f 8.47PM "	⑦ 1.58AM "	⑦ 1.58AM "
1914	Needles, Cal. (P.S.T.) Lv	8.55PM "	8.55PM "	2.05AM "	2.05AM "
2081	Barstow Ar	11.40PM Mon.	11.35PM "	5.00AM Tues.	5.00AM Tues.
	For complete schedule Barstow-San Francisco, see Table 7, page 9.				
0	Barstow Lv		11.55PM Mon.		
138	Bakersfield Lv		3.40AM Tues.		
249	Fresno Lv		5.45AM "		
440	Richmond Ar		10.00AM		
440	Richmond Lv		⊠10.05AM "		
448	Berkeley Lv		⊠10.30AM "		
451	Oakland Ar		⊠10.45AM "		
460	San Francisco Ar		⊠10.45AM Tues.		
2081	Barstow Lv	1.00AM Tues.		5.10AM Tues.	5.10AM Tues.
2135	Victorville Ar	f 1.45AM "		ⓐ 5.45AM "	ⓐ 5.45AM "
2163	San Bernardino Lv	3.20AM "		7.00AM "	7.00AM "
2188	Pomona Lv	4.20AM "		7.40AM "	7.40AM "
2213	Pasadena Ar	5.20AM "		8.25AM "	8.25AM "
2222	Los Angeles Ar	6.00AM Tues.		9.00AM Tues.	9.00AM Tues.
2222	Los Angeles Lv	7.30AM Tues.	TR. No. 74	11.00AM Tues.	11.00AM Tues.
	For complete schedule Los Angeles-San Diego, see Table 5, page 8.			TR. No. 76	TR. No. 76
2349	San Diego (P.S.T.) Ar	10.25AM Tues.		1.55PM Tues.	1.55PM Tues.

4

Eastbound Condensed Transcontinental Passenger Schedules

Miles	Table 2	No. 24 (See Note A) Daily Example	No. 2 San Francisco Chief (See Note A) Daily Example	No. 18 Super Chief Extra Fare Daily Example	No. 18 El Capitan Extra Fare Daily Example
0	San Diego, Cal. (P.S.T.) Lv	4.00PM Sun.			4.00PM Sun.
	For complete schedule San Diego-Los Angeles, see Table 5, page 8.				
127	Los Angeles Ar	6.55PM Sun.			6.55PM Sun.
0	Los Angeles Lv	9.00PM Sun.		7.30PM Sun.	7.30PM Sun.
9	Pasadena Lv	9.40PM "		8.00PM "	8.00PM "
34	Pomona Lv	10.20PM "		8.39PM "	8.39PM "
59	San Bernardino Lv	11.10PM "		9.12PM "	9.12PM "
106	Victorville Lv	12.35AM Mon.		10.33PM "	10.33PM "
142	Barstow Ar	1.10AM Mon.		11.10PM Sun.	11.10PM Sun.
	For complete schedule San Francisco-Barstow, see Table 7, page 9.				
0	San Francisco Lv		3.45PM Sun.		
9	Oakland Lv		3.45PM "		
12	Berkeley Lv		4.00PM "		
20	Richmond Ar		4.25PM "		
20	Richmond Lv		4.30PM "		
211	Fresno Lv		8.05PM "		
322	Bakersfield Ar		10.05PM Sun.		
460	Barstow Ar		1.30AM Mon.		
142	Barstow Lv	2.00AM	1.45AM Mon.	11.20PM Mon.	11.20PM Mon.
307	Needles Cal. (P.S.T.) Lv	5.10AM	4.20AM	2.00AM Mon.	2.00AM Mon.
368	Kingman, Ariz. (M.S.T.) Lv	7.40AM	6.31AM	4.14AM "	4.14AM "
457	Seligman Lv	9.25AM	8.15AM	5.55AM "	5.55AM "
541	Flagstaff Ar	11.15AM	9.55AM Mon.	7.33AM Mon.	7.33AM Mon.
	For complete schedules Flagstaff-Grand Canyon and Flagstaff-Phoenix, see Table 6, page 8.				
647	Phoenix Ar	2.55PM Mon.	2.55PM Mon.	1.30PM Mon.	1.30PM Mon.
614	Grand Canyon Ar	6.20PM "	11.35AM Mon.	10.05AM Mon.	10.05AM Mon.
	Phoenix Lv	8.10AM Sun.			
	Grand Canyon Lv	7.00PM Sun.	7.00PM Sun.	7.00PM Sun.	7.00PM Sun.
541	Flagstaff Lv	11.15AM	9.55AM Mon.	7.33AM Mon.	7.33AM Mon.
599	Winslow Lv	12.30PM	11.25AM	8.50AM "	8.50AM "
632	Holbrook, Ariz. Lv	1.00PM	11.55AM		
726	Gallup, N.M. Lv	2.20PM	1.20PM	10.37AM "	10.37AM "
788	Grants Lv	3.20PM	2.23PM Mon.		
816	Laguna Lv	3.45PM			
871	Belen Ar		3.45PM Mon.		
871	Belen Lv		4.05PM Mon.		
887	Albuquerque Ar	5.00PM		1.10PM Mon.	1.10PM Mon.
887	Albuquerque Lv	5.10PM	*For complete schedule Belen-Wichita, see Table 4, page 8.*	1.20PM "	1.20PM "
903	Bernalillo Lv	5.30PM			
954	Lamy Ar	6.25PM Mon.			
972	Santa Fe, N.M. Lv			2.25PM Mon.	2.25PM Mon.
954	Lamy Lv	6.25PM		2.25PM Mon.	2.25PM Mon.
1019	Las Vegas Lv	8.15PM		4.13PM "	4.13PM "
1128	Raton, N.M. Lv	10.15PM		6.05PM "	6.05PM "
1150	Trinidad, Colo. Lv	11.15PM Mon.		7.01PM "	7.01PM "
1233	La Junta Lv	12.40AM Tues.		8.15PM Mon.	8.15PM Mon.
	For complete schedule La Junta-Denver, see Table 11, page 10.				
1415	Denver Ar	8.40AM Tues.		A12.30AM Tues.	A12.30AM Tues.
1415	Denver Lv			A 3.30PM Mon.	A 3.30PM Mon.
1233	La Junta, Colo. Lv	1.00AM Tues.		8.25PM Mon.	8.25PM Mon.
1251	Las Animas, Colo. Lv	1.22AM "			
1284	Lamar, Colo. Lv	1.55AM "			
1333	Syracuse, Kan. Lv	2.41AM "			
1362	Lakin Lv	3.07AM "			
1385	Garden City (M.S.T.) Lv	3.30AM "		9.08PM Mon.	9.08PM Mon.
1435	Dodge City (C.S.T.) Lv	5.35AM "			
1456	Kinsley Lv	6.01AM "			
1555	Hutchinson, Kan. Lv	7.20AM Tues.		10.26PM Mon.	10.26PM Mon.
1112	Clovis, N.M. Lv		H10.15PM Mon.	12.23AM Tues.	12.23AM Tues.
1215	Amarillo, Tex. Lv		12.25AM Tues.	1.58AM Tues.	1.58AM Tues.
1527	Wellington, Kan. Lv		6.10AM "		
1561	Wichita Ar		7.05AM "		
1588	Newton Ar	8.05AM Tues.	7.40AM "	2.35AM Tues.	2.35AM Tues.
1588	Newton Lv	8.15AM "	7.50AM "	2.40AM "	2.40AM "
1661	Emporia Lv	9.25AM "	9.00AM "	3.45AM "	3.45AM "
1687	Osage City Lv	9.55AM "			
1722	Topeka Lv	10.40AM "	10.15AM "		
1749	Lawrence, Kan. Lv	11.15AM "	10.45AM "		
1773	Kansas City, Mo. Ar	12.15PM Tues.	11.45AM Tues.	5.35AM Tues.	5.35AM Tues.
	For complete schedule Kansas City-Tulsa, see Table 3, page 7.				
2029	Tulsa, Okla. Lv	7.15AM Tues.			
1773	Kansas City, Mo. Lv	12.30PM Tues.	12.15PM Tues.	5.50AM Tues.	5.50AM Tues.
1837	Carrollton Lv	1.44PM "	1.24PM "		
1876	Marceline Lv	2.20PM "	1.58PM "		
1911	La Plata, Mo. Lv	2.35PM "	2.35PM "		
1990	Ft. Madison, Iowa Lv	4.25PM "	3.55PM "	9.15AM "	9.15AM "
2045	Galesburg, Ill. Lv	5.25PM "	4.50PM "	10.10AM "	10.10AM "
2093	Chillicothe, Ill. Lv	6.20PM "	5.35PM "	10.55AM "	10.55AM "
2133	Streator Lv	7.08PM "	6.15PM "	f11.35AM "	f11.35AM "
2165	Coal City Lv	7.40PM "			
2185	Joliet Lv	8.04PM "	7.05PM "	12.25PM "	12.25PM "
2223	Chicago, Ill. (C.S.T.) Ar	9.00PM Tues.	8.00PM Tues.	1.30PM Tues.	1.30PM Tues.

5   6

In July 1970, the Santa Fe issued its last public timetable. There were three sets of daily trains, namely, Nos. 1 and 2 (The San Francisco Chief), Nos. 17 and 18 (Super Chief and El Capitan), and Nos. 23 and 24 (the former Grand Canyon Limited). Santa Fe Railway.

Behind the Lamy station, the local train stands ready to take passengers from the main line to Santa Fe. The coal tower is in the distance. The year is 1910. Percy Jones, Jr. photograph.

Fred Harvey's restaurants and hotels along the Santa Fe were famous for their fine service. The Alvarado Hotel, the Harvey House in Albuquerque, is pictured in 1910. Percy Jones, Jr., photograph.

When Amtrak took over passenger service in 1971, only one daily train was operating between Chicago and Los Angeles via the Santa Fe Railway. This train is in northern New Mexico. **National Railroad Passenger Corporation.**

of a premeditated plan to cause a missed train connection. But Fred Harvey's organization was ready for such mishaps; a tow truck with a long cable would be assigned to troublesome spots to pull buses through the errant waters to facilitate on-time arrival at Lamy.

In 1931, the Indian Detours were purchased by Hunter Clarkson, the former manager, and since 1968, when they were sold, operations have been carried on by The Gray Line.

Pecos River Valley

From Trinidad, Colorado and Southern lines run southeast to Fort Worth, Texas, a distance of almost 600 miles, and from the same point the Santa Fe goes south to El Paso. Linking El Paso and Fort Worth, the T&P forms the base of a huge triangle, enclosing an area of thousands of square miles which did not gain railroad transportation until long after the peripheral lines had been well established. In New Mexico the triangle embraced the Sacramento Mountains, much of the drainage of the 700-mile-long Pecos River, the Permian Basin and the Llano Estacado or Staked Plains, at one time a grim and forbidding plateau east of the Pecos River.

Various railroad proposals had been entertained from time to time. Among the earlier prospects was the Colorado and New Mexico Railroad of David H. Moffat of the later Moffat Tunnel fame. Projected from Denver south to Texas along the Pecos River in 1870, it did not materialize because Congress would not sanction a land grant.

Two remarkable men set out to tame and develop the valley by building railroads and irrigation systems. One was James John Hagerman who amassed a fortune in Great Lakes iron mines only to be forced into retirement at the age of 44 because of broken health. Moving to Colorado Springs, he busied himself with the Colorado Midland Railroad but in 1889, he was ready to listen to a Pecos Valley rancher, Charles B. Eddy, expound on the possibilities of irrigating the area and then to link the developed land with the outside world by a railroad.

The pioneer railroad of what became a major enterprise was The Pecos Valley Railway organized by Hagerman in 1890 to build north from Pecos (City), on the main line of the Texas & Pacific, into New Mexico to the lands to be subjected to irrigation. The almost brand-new town of Eddy (now Carlsbad) had been formed the year before, but early in 1891 it was linked to the outside world by 89 miles of railroad. Roswell, an older community 70 miles farther north, greeted its first trains three years later.

It was necessary to pour large sums of money into the construction of the railroad and the irrigation canals and dams. The depression of 1893 which closed the doors to the flow of bank funds and a flood which destroyed a major dam struck down the efforts of the two men. After they split apart in 1895, Hagerman took on the job of building up his line to make it saleable to the Santa Fe. With some financial assistance from

Establishing the first train into Roswell requires a clarification for there were two, and both arrived the same day, October 6, 1894. A construction train, with a private car on the end, stopped at the edge of town in order to permit a special three-car train with people gathered from the valley to be the first to enter Roswell and to celebrate the event. James D. Shinkle Collection.

For decades the Santa Fe offered daily passenger service over the Pecos Valley line from Chicago as far as Carlsbad. Before World War I, a Pullman ran through from Newton, Kansas. In the twenties this was supplanted by a Pullman run from Carlsbad to Albuquerque via Clovis. With the onslaught of the Great Depression, a motor car was substituted on an Amarillo-Carlsbad daylight run. The increasing popularity of the Carlsbad caverns brought back the steam train on an overnight connection with the Chicago-Los Angeles Scout, and a Pullman that laid over in Carlsbad—first, on a run from Waynoka, Oklahoma to Belen; and later, on a run from Chicago to Albuquerque. This arrangement expired early in the 1950s, and the motor outfit returned. A typical consist is shown above, with Motor M-190, at Carlsbad in 1960. The Carlsbad-Pecos end of the line never enjoyed heavy passenger travel and only supported a mixed train for many years. It is shown in two 1959–60 views (left): leaving Carlsbad; and arriving at midnight in Pecos, Texas. All photographs, Fred M. Springer.

that road, Hagerman formed a new company, The Pecos Valley and Northeastern Railway, and built 113 miles (including one straight track of 26 miles) from Roswell and the valley to Portales, Cameo and Texico. At this point, he continued to build in Texas under a different corporate name until he connected with the lines of the Santa Fe at Amarillo. Completed in the spring of 1899, control of this railroad had already passed to the Santa Fe.

Traffic generated along this line reflected the changes brought about by irrigation. The open-slatted livestock cars, taking cattle from the sprawling range to the markets, gave way to cars carrying alfalfa and then to ice-cooled cars hauling peaches and tomatoes.

Passenger traffic generated along the line supported nothing more than a local train or motor car, religiously stopping at each station for mail, express packages and the occasional travelers. But the discovery of the Carlsbad Caverns in 1901 and particularly the formation of a national park in 1930 brought improved passenger service to the Pecos Valley. To accommodate the flow of tourists, one line of Pullman sleeping cars operating between Chicago and Los Angeles was sidetracked at Clovis and sent down to Carlsbad during the night where buses met the passengers the following morning for the 30-mile drive to the Caverns. After an underground tour, the tourists were returned to Carlsbad to board their waiting Pullman for the return that evening to Clovis where the car was switched into the main line train.

It was the discovery of potash, for many years Santa Fe's largest single commodity of traffic, near the Pecos Valley branch and more recently the development of a sulphur deposit, that turned a once struggling railroad into an important part of a major system.

Potash and Sulphur

When James Snowden and Henry McSweeney sank a test well about 20 miles east of Carlsbad in 1925, they were disappointed not to find oil. Instead, their epic well opened a whole new industry in New Mexico for down 1,000 feet in-

Potash discoveries in the Pecos Valley began with core drilling by the American Potash Co. and others in the 1920s. U.S. Geological Survey photograph.

dications of potash were found in the form of sylvite ore. Although there had been potash found in the United States previously, it was not of commercial stature and most had to be imported from Europe.

Further drilling convinced the two oil men to form the American Potash Company (later called the U.S. Potash Company and still later, U.S. Borax & Chemical Corporation) to proceed in the mining of potash. The Pacific Coast Borax Company joined the venture in 1930 and, from this affiliation, a new narrow-gauge railroad was born, perhaps the last built in the United States and certainly the last in New Mexico. The

The United Potash Company had extensive works at Carlsbad. The three-foot railroad system, for a long time steam powered, drew rail enthusiasts to witness the operations. From one Arizona copper railroad, the Morenci Southern Railway, it acquired an outside-frame locomotive with a 2-8-0 wheel arrangement. In later years, this locomotive, No. 3, was donated to the Southern California Chapter of the R. & L.H.S. **Both photos, U.S. Borax Company, 1956.**

36-inch gauge was not a matter of chance; there was good reason, namely a surplus railroad. The borax mine of the Pacific Coast Borax Company at Ryan, California, had become exhausted and the narrow-gauge Death Valley Railroad, an affiliated company with almost no other source of traffic, had no alternative but abandonment in 1931. The motive power (two Baldwins), ore cars, the motor car and rails were sent to New Mexico to begin a new life.

The AT&SF built a five-mile standard-gauge spur eastward from Loving (seven miles south of Carlsbad) to the U.S. Potash refinery. Production began in September 1932 as the former D.V.R.R. equipment brought potash from the mine over the 16-

mile railroad to the refinery. In 1956, after the narrow gauge
had turned to diesel power, one of the steam locomotives was
brought back to California's Death Valley where it was put on
display at the Furnace Creek Ranch.

Though times were tough in 1933, the Potash Corporation
of America and the Santa Fe joined in the construction of another branch line to their potash mine, 20 miles northeast of
Carlsbad. Later this spur was pushed north to the Southwest
Potash Company (American Metal Company).

The Santa Fe spur at Loving was extended ten miles in 1939
to serve the Union Potash & Chemical Company (now International Minerals & Chemical Corporation), paralleling the nar-

The steam locomotives, after providing useful service for many years, were replaced by narrow-gauge diesel locomotives. Nos. 4 and 6 are shown here. **Fred M. Springer photograph, 1959.**

row-gauge line for part of the way. Other spurs have been built to the potash works of National and Duval. In all, there are now seven producers in this area.

The original potash operation of U.S. Borax & Chemical was closed in November 1967 and subsequently was sold to a new group. It is now being operated under the name of the U.S. Potash & Chemical Company.

Completed in July 1969 was the latest section of railroad construction in that part of New Mexico. Near the confluence of Delaware Creek (River) and the Pecos River, about 30 miles south of Carlsbad, the Santa Fe began construction of a new railroad on March 24, 1969 to the sulphur deposits being opened by Duval Corporation near Rustler Springs, Texas. Most of the 25-mile branch is in Texas but the connection with the Pecos River branch and the four-mile change on the latter branch are in New Mexico. When in full operation, four unit-trains, each with 66 tank cars will make the 1,840-mile round trip between the sulphur mine and Galveston, Texas.

Hagerman envisioned the Pecos Valley as an agricultural empire, but today's cash crops for the Santa Fe Railway are potash and sulphur. To serve Duval sulphur deposits at Rustler Springs, Texas, a 25-mile line was built form Pecos Junction, N.M. in 1969. Using trains of 66 tank cars, the Santa Fe hauled molten sulphur 925 miles to Galveston, Texas for export. **Santa Fe Railway.**

New Mexico Central Railway

As this century began, two financial adventurers from Pennsylvania, Francis J. Torrance and William H. Andrews, decided to enter central New Mexico, the private transportation domain of the Santa Fe and the Rio Grande. The way of entry was by a standard-gauge railroad over 100 miles long which turned out to be a costly venture for these two men and their associates.

Torrance, for many years a vice president of the Standard Sanitary Manufacturing Company (plumbing supplies) was also active in Pennsylvania politics. Andrews, a merchant in Ohio and Pennsylvania, had also engaged in railroad construction. Additionally he had been a member of the Pennsylvania legislature, an interest he carried with him when he moved to

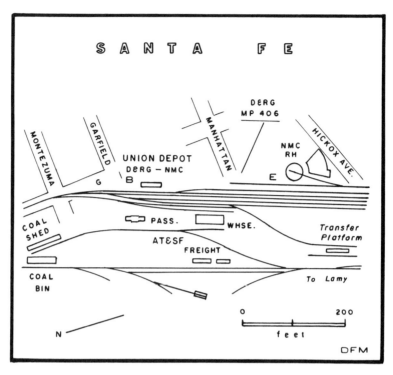

When the Santa Fe Central (later called the New Mexico Central) built its own railroad into Santa Fe, it joined the D&RG in the construction of the Union Station. To accommodate both narrow-gauge and standard-gauge cars, three rails were necessary from a point 350 feet north of Montezuma Avenue, through jointly owned station grounds (B-E) and terminating at Hickox Avenue. Additionally, the D&RG owned a third rail on Track 14 of the NMC extending 5,691 feet to a stockyard southwest of Santa Fe.

New Mexico in 1900. Besides mining in Sierra County and railroading, he was a member of the Council and later a delegate in Congress from New Mexico.

The original company, incorporated in December 1900, carried the rather ambitious name of Santa Fe, Albuquerque & Pacific Railroad Company which was changed to the Santa Fe Central Railway the following July. In the same month as the name change, the affiliated Albuquerque Eastern Railway was formed.

During 1901, as the El Paso & Rock Island was moving northeasterly to meet the Rock Island at Santa Rosa, the Santa

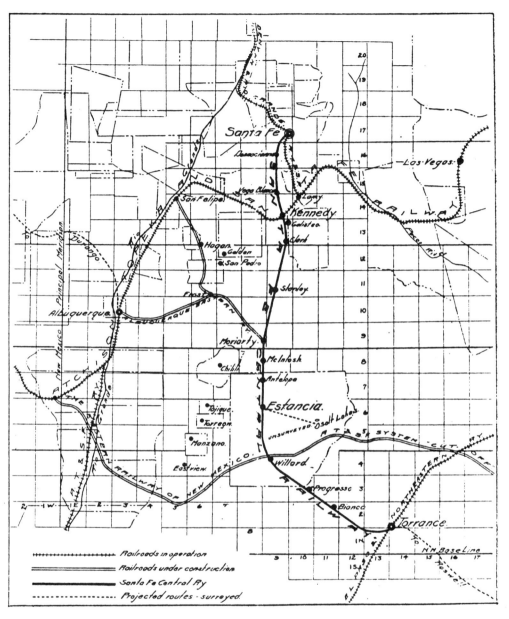

A map of the Santa Fe Central System, circa 1908, indicated an ambitious management. The Albuquerque Eastern Railway, an affiliate, had two lines "under construction." One would have gone from Moriarty to Albuquerque and then linked Frost with Hagan and San Felipe. After some grading, work was suspended permanently. Some years later, the Rio Grande Eastern built a railroad to Hagan. Denver Public Library.

The last spike of track laying of the Santa Fe Central took place at Kennedy on August 13, 1903. The Harris track-laying machine, widely used in railroad construction at that time, is to the left of the crowd. A neighbor hitched his team to the surrey to watch the event.

Fe Central decided to join forces with them by providing a 116-mile link with the Territorial capital. The EP&RI evidenced its sanction of the proposal by naming the junction "Torrance."

Contracts were reported to have been let in the fall of 1901 with the full expectation that trains would be running to Santa Fe by July 4, 1902. This might have happened but for the fact that the commencement of grading was delayed until the spring of 1902. By that summer several hundred teams were at work. An impressive townsite was laid out at Mr. Moriarty's ranch where the Albuquerque Eastern Railway was to join the Santa Fe Central.

Timbers for many of the bridges were arriving by the D&RG and by December the grade was completed for the 50 miles south of Santa Fe and for ten miles west of Torrance, leaving the "easier portion" to be done. When the first locomotive arrived at Torrance in January 1903 it had no place to go except back and forth on the SFC yard tracks there.

During 1903 the gap in the railroad grade was closed, ties were distributed and the popular Harris track laying machine

ON AUGUST 20, 1903,

—THE—

Santa Fe Central Railway

IN CONNECTION WITH THE

Will Open a New Passenger and Freight Line Between

SANTA FE, N. M.,

AND

VIA
TORRANCE **EL PASO, TEXAS,**

THUS IS THE LONG-WISHED-FOR EVENT ACCOMPLISHED.

Call on local agents for full information regarding
this new line, the country it runs through. Freight
and Passenger Rates and other desired particulars.

A. N. BROWN, G. F. & P. A., E. P. N. E. SYSTEM, EL PASO, TEXAS.

THE DENVER & RIO GRANDE SYSTEM

Denver & Rio Grande, Rio Grande Western, Rio
Grande & Santa Fe and Rio Grande
Southern Railroads.

THE POPULAR LINE TO

Colorado Springs, Pueblo, Cripple Creek, Leadville,
Glenwood Springs, Aspen, Grand Junction, Salt
Lake City, Ogden, Butte, Helena, San Francisco,
Los Angeles, Portland. Tacoma, and Seattle. Also
Reaches all the Principal Towns and Mining Camps
in Colorado, Utah and New Mexico.

THE TOURIST'S FAVORITE ROUTE

To all Mountain Resorts

*A newspaper advertisement announced the opening of the new
railroad a week after the last spike was driven. The little road
offered connections to almost everywhere.*

A photographer climbed the flour mill in Estancia in September 1919 to record this view of the town and the railroad shops. H. J. Maxwell Collection.

The Union Station in Santa Fe, once jointly owned by the D&RG and NMC, had long been used for other purposes when this photograph was made in 1969.

was stringing the rails in place. Finally the great day came, for the Santa Fe Central was completed on August 13, 1903 with the new route to El Paso being opened a week later. W. S. Hopewell, the general manager, gathered a party of 25 and took them down to Kennedy in a caboose to watch Santa Fe's Mayor Sparks drive the last spike, appropriately made of New Mexico silver. The spike was donated by S. Spitz, manufacturing jewelers of Santa Fe, the same firm which also fashioned the famed silver filigree passes of the Rio Grande Southern. Kennedy, named for Arthur Kennedy of Pittsburgh, Chairman of the Board, was the point where crossing of the AT&SF was made.

Late in 1903, the Union Depot of the Santa Fe Central and the D&RG was completed in Santa Fe. (This brick structure, still standing about 100 feet east of the AT&SF depot, was about $2/3$ of a mile south of the old Rio Grande depot.)

Work was also under way on the Albuquerque Eastern Railway line to Albuquerque via Tijeras Pass but was halted on the 43-mile line after the initial eight miles from Moriarty had been built. A branch was surveyed from Frost, 17 miles west of Moriarty on the AE Railway to San Felipe on the AT&SF via the Hagan coal fields. Other branches were seriously projected from Estancia to the Salt Lakes and to the smelter at San Pedro. Preliminary surveys were made in one direction to Durango, Colorado, and in the other direction to Roswell, New Mexico, and there was some visionary talk of extending both ends of the Santa Fe Central to join Salt Lake City with the T&P at Big Springs, Texas, as a route to the Gulf.

There were excursions to Estancia and other places but the great dreams were not to be realized as the traffic generated along the SFC and AE was insufficient to support the railroad. The two railroads were consolidated in 1908 to form the New Mexico Central Railroad and the following year a contract was signed to resume work on the Albuquerque branch, a project which failed to materialize because of the lack of funds.

Things went from bad to worse, a receiver was appointed in 1910 and by 1915 train service was reduced to a tri-weekly operation requiring nearly eight hours for the 116 miles, lunch being provided at Stanley. Finally, in 1918, a new company, the New Mexico Central *Railway*, emerged but the problems stemming from the lack of tonnage remained the same. In an

Type of Gasoline Cars used between Torrance and Santa Fe, New Mexico

NEW SERVICE

VIA THE

GOLDEN STATE LIMITED

AND

NEW MEXICO CENTRAL RY.

BETWEEN

SANTA FE, NEW MEXICO

AND

KANSAS CITY, ST. LOUIS, CHICAGO

Mon. Wed. Fri.	Tues. Thurs. Sat.			Mon. Wed. Fri.	Tues. Thurs. Sat.
9.35 am	10.45 am	Lv._____SANTA FE_____Ar.		1.35 pm	3.45 pm
5.40 pm	5.40 pm	Ar._____ KANSAS CITY ____Lv.		9.05 am	9.05 am
7.25 am	7.25 am	Ar._____ST. LOUIS_____Lv.		9.03 pm	9.03 pm
9.15 am	9.15 am	Ar._____CHICAGO _____Lv.		6.30 pm	6.30 pm

See page 14 for detailed schedule between Santa Fe and Torrance, N. M.

In its struggle for survival, the New Mexico Central purchased the Mack railbus which, effective June 1, 1924, provided faster service three times a week from Santa Fe to Torrance with Chicago connections. Even with this improvement, the local line was no match for the Santa Fe's fine trains from nearby Lamy. Fred M. Springer Collection.

The shop force of the reorganized New Mexico Central Railway suspended work for this photograph on April 3, 1919. The third man from the right, in the front row, is Claude A. Smith, master mechanic. Herman J. Maxwell, the man who collected these photographs, is in the second row, first man from the left. **H. J. Maxwell Collection.**

effort to add more traffic, the previously proposed line toward Durango came up again; this time, however, the objective was Farmington, New Mexico. Initially, the New Mexico Central contemplated building about 100 miles of railroad from Santa Fe northwesterly to Gallina. From this area, it was hoped that lumber, coal, livestock and farm products would yield additional traffic. ICC approval for construction of this branch was obtained in 1923 but nothing more was accomplished.

Net losses in ever increasing amounts were recorded in the early 1920s and the future existence of the entire railroad was at best, marginal. The Santa Fe agreed to buy the railroad for

The New Mexico Central had a mixture of second-hand locomotives. This one, built for the El Paso and Northeastern by Baldwin, was acquired in 1919. The curved cab window confirms prior EP&NE ownership. Photograph H. J. Maxwell Collection.

$700,000 cash in 1926 and the property came under its control. Three years later the segments from Kennedy to Santa Fe and from Torrance to Willard were abandoned reducing the mileage of the former NMC to one-half its original length. Further reductions were made in 1939 and 1943 so that the remainder consisted of the 28-mile sergment between Estancia and Calvert (Moriarty). For some years this branch was served by the "Calvert Turn" until it made its last run on September 20, 1974.

The principal geographic reminders are the town and county of Torrance named for a man who spent most of his time in Pennsylvania. It is a little ironic that William Henry Andrews, who did much work in the battle for statehood, who was president of the Santa Fe Central Railway and a resident of New Mexico for two decades, was honored only by a small town at his mine near Hillsboro which has been a ghost town for many years.

SOUTHERN PACIFIC TRANSPORTATION COMPANY

The Southern Pacific Railroad Company of New Mexico

The history of the construction of the Southern Pacific in New Mexico is brief for it was accomplished without problems—the 167 miles across the territory were built in less than one year. The story of its operations over a period of more than 100 years is another matter. So are the stories of the construction of the lines making up the El Paso & Southwestern which brought the total Southern Pacific mileage in New Mexico to almost 1,000 miles when the merger took place in 1924. The EP&SW mileage was augmented by several acquisitions, the El Paso & Northeastern being the largest and, like the EP&SW, forms a separate chapter in this book.

The purpose of the railroad was to connect California with the Gulf of Mexico; New Mexico was a link between Arizona and Texas. The "Big Four," Stanford, Crocker, Huntington and Hopkins (until his death in 1878), were pushing their Southern Pacific along the southern edge of the country, forming a different corporation for each state, generally with similar names.

The Southern Pacific's Lordsburg station was a long and low structure. The Wells Fargo Express was located in the next building.

The Southern Pacific Railroad Company (of New Mexico) was incorporated April 14, 1879.

By entering Arizona at Yuma on September 30, 1877, SP was the first railroad in that territory. After pausing at Yuma for almost a year, the men picked up their tools and built to Casa Grande where again they suspended work until January 1880 when construction was resumed. Tucson celebrated the arrival of the railroad on March 20, 1880 and by the end of September track layers were driving spikes in New Mexico. The Chinese graders kept moving ahead and the track layers followed closely behind. Trains began serving the new town of Lordsburg on October 18, 1880 and Deming on December 15, 1880. El Paso greeted its first railroad when the Southern Pacific, after bridging the Rio Grande, arrived in that Texas town on May 19, 1881. The line was operated under lease by the Central Pacific until March 1, 1885, and the Southern Pacific Company thereafter.

Already the Southern Pacific had formed the western part of the second transcontinental railroad when the Santa Fe reached Deming on March 8, 1881. The Texas & Pacific, now revitalized with the strong backing of financier Jay Gould, was making

*When the Southern Pacific and the Santa Fe met at Deming in
1881, the second transcontinental railroad was born. In this photograph taken by the Buehmans not too long after the connection
was made, a number of men have converged on the Wells Fargo
& Company's Express office to collect their shipments. The building to the east, hiding the joint station, is the baggage house. The
flatcar bears the letters "C.P." for the Central Pacific and the
locomotive is No. 60 of the SP of Arizona. To the left rear are cars
on the Santa Fe tracks.* Arizona Historical Society.

rapid strides in its westward march from Fort Worth. With equal
determination, the Southern Pacific forces were pushing east
from El Paso; both coveted the one logical pass to the east. SP
won the race when it met the T&P at Sierra Blanca, 90 miles
east of El Paso, on November 25, 1881, thus forming part of
the third transcontinental rail route across the nation.

The T&P, earlier that year, feeling that its rights in New
Mexico had been usurped by the SP, took the matter to court.
The dispute was resolved by the famed Huntington-Gould
agreement under which the T&P gained access to El Paso over
SP tracks. The SP, under the name of its Texas affiliate, The
Galveston, Harrisburg and San Antonio Railway, continued to

The Southern Pacific crosses the Continental Divide at Mile Post 1176.7, 28 miles east of Lordsburg, with an elevation of 4,584 feet.

The Sunset Limited passes through a cut at Lizard, ten miles west of El Paso, in May 1926.

Near Steins Mountain, a part of the Peloncillo Mountains, the Southern Pacific operated a ballast quarry for many years. This work train, near Steins in September 1910, was headed by a 2-8-0 locomotive of Baldwin manufacture. No. 2814 spent its final years on the SPdeM.

build eastward to the Pecos River where it met other affiliated forces on January 12, 1883, thus completing a through line from San Francisco to New Orleans. (Ownership of the GH&SA property was transferred to the Texas and New Orleans Railroad in 1934 which, in turn, was conveyed to the Southern Pacific Company in 1961.)

One of the reasons justifying the Gadsden Purchase of 1853 was that it offered the lowest crossing of the Continental Divide. The early Pacific Railroad Surveys included this crossing among the several proposed routes and William Hood laid out the line for the SP to cross the Divide at 4,584 feet with a few $1^{1}/_{2}\%$ grades.

Traffic for this portion of the railroad came from such mining towns as Shakespeare (near Lordsburg) and the livestock trade but the main support came from interstate shipments. When the line was first opened and for many years thereafter, one daily scheduled passenger train could accommodate all the local and through traffic offered, in spite of active promotion

The Blue Streak Merchandise, *the fast Cotton Belt-Southern Pacific train, was photographed in 1959 as it passed through Peloncillo Mountains and approached the Arizona line.*

The Southern Pacific Railroad Company of New Mexico   **65**

Once quarried, the rock went through a crusher to reduce it to ballast size.

of the "Sunset Route," as this line was designated. Eastbound, the *New Orleans Express,* and westbound, the *Sunset Express* ran between San Francisco and New Orleans. Although the "express" trains stopped at every station, there were two additional daily mixed trains operating each way across New Mexico to El Paso.

The *Sunset Limited* began as a supplementary weekly train in the winter of 1894 and ran seasonally once or twice a week until 1902 when it became a daily train, only to be discontinued entirely after two years. Service was not resumed until 1912 when it ran as a weekly train followed by regular daily operation the next year. With a fleet of 76 stainless steel cars, the

Southern Pacific's westbound Californian *was just leaving Lordsburg in December 1946. Locomotive No. 4434 is cloaked in the colorful red and orange sheathing to match the popular* Daylight *trains of California.* A. C. Phelps photograph.

Sunset became a streamliner with considerable fanfare in 1950. Another name train on this route was the *Argonaut.*

Operations of this section of the Southern Pacific included a history of the usual events such as the difficulty of obtaining adequate water for the steam locomotives on one hand and too much water from desert cloudbursts damaging bridges and grades on the other. There were hold-ups—a locomotive engineer was killed in one of the first railroad robberies in the Southwest near Gage—and, until Geronimo was subdued in 1886, track walkers were sometimes the victims of Apaches. There were fires destroying station buildings and nature brought its share of problems with temperature changes from the heat of summer to winter snows.

For many years SP locomotives were supplied with coal from Raton, New Mexico, but in 1901, after the successful use of fuel oil in California, oil tanks began appearing at various points along the Sunset Route. In October of that year, an oil-

Near Lordsburg, the SP's affiliate, the Cotton Belt, loaned power for this freight train with four cattle cars immediately behind the tender, a scene which has not been possible for many years as livestock largely moves by highway carrier. Steve Maguire photograph.

burning locomotive, No. 1661, made the first run of its kind between Tucson and Lordsburg. The engineer, Tom Falvey, reported that it was easy to keep clean and that it pulled as well as a coal burner. Other enginemen were jealous, particularly when the word got around that the cab of the oil burner had a carpet on the floor!

With the El Paso & Southwestern merger in 1924, the SP inherited a fleet of coal-fired locomotives. For a long time they were in use on the Rio Grande Division as far west as Tucson. (Coal chutes were built at such points as Tucson, Lordsburg, etc.) The SP had bought nothing but oil-fired locomotives for many years; a policy which was altered twice in the pre-diesel days. In 1939 when the SP bought 28 AC-8, cab-in-front, oil-fired locomotives from Baldwin, they also bought a dozen AC-

SP No. 3504, taking on water at Lordsburg, was one of the ten-coal burners purchased from the Boston & Maine in August 1945 to meet the critical demand for motive power. The unusual Coffin feed-water heater is mounted on the outside front of the firebox. A. C. Phelps photograph, 1946.

9 (2-8-8-4) coal-burning locomotives from Lima. These had the cab in the usual position, behind the boiler and fire-box, and were numbered 3800–3811. At the close of World War II, the SP also bought ten Berkshire (2-8-4) Lima-built, coal-burning locomotives from the Boston & Maine for use on the Rio Grande Division.

The coal mines at Dawson, which had been the source of fuel for the Rio Grande Division for many years, entered a difficult period after World War II. Sales of coal, which had been running around one million tons annually back in 1927, faced overwhelming competition from oil and natural gas and in later years were less than half the former figure. Rising costs and exhaustion of the coal fields caused the mines to close on April 28, 1950. The steam locomotives were then changed to burn fuel oil and the AC-9s spent their remaining years on SP's Modoc Line in eastern California, while the Berkshires were used elsewhere.

Abandonment of the Dawson branch followed, the last 18 miles from Dawson to French going in 1952 and the remaining 114 miles ten years later.

For many years an increasing share of traffic between Tucson and El Paso was moving over the North Line (Lordsburg) rather than via the South Line which was 29 miles longer. Very little traffic originated east of Douglas and studies indicated that the operating savings from the abandonment of 208.9 miles of railroad between Douglas and Anapra, New Mexico (six miles west of El Paso) would offset the cost of the longer haul of copper anodes from Douglas through Benson to the refinery at El Paso. Following ICC approval, operations of this line ceased December 20, 1961 but, pending the outcome of litigation that followed, tracks and facilities remained in place until 1963, when the courts upheld the ICC order. (Anapra to El Paso, part of a long established double-track operation, remained in service.)

Centralized Traffic Control was first installed on Southern Pacific in 1930. Additional sections were budgeted as required by increased traffic and the availability of funds. CTC, generally increasing the capacity of single track, is now in place on many parts of the SP, including from Los Angeles to El Paso and to Sierra Blanca, Texas, the last section having been placed in service in 1960.

After World War II, SP replaced the rolling stock of its main line passenger trains with sparkling new equipment. The greatest pride was taken in the new *Sunset Limited*, for which 78 stainless steel cars were ordered from Budd in June 1948. This equipment provided for the operation of five trains between Los Angeles, El Paso and New Orleans plus a sixth for a shopping margin. When the cars were delivered two years later, they were welcomed with extensive promotions, including a new color called "Sunset Pink."

In the next two decades, steadily declining passenger traffic brought a change in the *Sunset* schedules from a daily operation to a three times a week, effective October 1, 1970. At the same time, a through sleeping car from Los Angeles to New Orleans, Washington and New York was instituted. When Amtrak took over the operation of most of the nation's passenger trains on May 1, 1971, the same tri-weekly *Sunset* operation continued. For a time, the transcontinental sleeping car also continued in operation but, in more recent years, it has been replaced with a through Los Angeles–New Orleans–Chicago car.

El Paso and Northeastern
Railroad System

Everybody wanted to build a railroad to White Oaks, or so it would appear from a reading of old newspapers and formal filings of incorporation in the territorial capital. White Oaks, located just south of the center of New Mexico, not far from Carrizozo, had its real beginnings in 1879 when three prospectors discovered gold at what became the Homestake claim. A rush of would-be miners soon followed, a hotel (with board at $4.00 per week) was established in February 1880, even before the usual whiskey shops or gambling enterprises appeared, a rather remarkable order of development for a frontier mining town. The Old Abe and other mines of the district are reported to have yielded almost $3,000,000 in gold ore.

Gold mining was one reason to build a railroad into the district from Las Vegas or Albuquerque, but promoters based in El Paso found the coal deposits at White Oaks a far more enticing reason. White Oaks coal, they felt, would be cheaper than coal from other mines in New Mexico and would provide cheaper fuel, the key to the city's growth. (It should be remembered that nearby petroleum and natural gas fields were still many decades away from discovery and full exploitation.)

At least five different railroads were seriously projected to span the 160 miles from El Paso to White Oaks during a period of 15 years before one soundly financed company accomplished the task. Each serious project had one thing in common: two companies had to be incorporated, one in New Mexico and one in Texas to comply with the laws of the latter state.

Though the names of the proposed railroads varied, many of the same names of sponsors appeared in one or more ventures. Among them was Joseph Magoffin of the State National Bank and later mayor of El Paso. One organization, the El Paso, St. Louis and Chicago Railway and Telegraph Company, formed in 1885, left a physical legacy of five miles of graded roadbed for the next effort three years later building under the name of the Kansas City, El Paso and Mexico Railroad.

Heading this company was H. L. Newman, who joined forces with Morris R. Locke & Company, the construction firm that had just previously finished the short line into Phoenix, Arizona. The grading subcontract was handled in part by the Detwiler brothers, who had the experience gained from forming the previous grade, and H. C. Park. Assisting the project were local El Paso businessmen who promised to advance two $50,000 loans if the construction was accomplished according to a specified schedule.

There was no formal celebration on September 3, 1888 when work began, but a number of doubting men showed up at Kansas and Eleventh Streets (El Paso) to be convinced that grading was actually a reality.

This enterprise was faced with right of way problems. Mr. Frank B. Cotton of Boston had a real estate development along the route of the railroad. Preliminary negotiations for a mutually satisfactory right of way had been concluded with the agent, Major Rand, but when Mr. Locke sought confirmation of these arrangements from Mr. Cotton in Boston, he was emphatically informed that the Boston man was less than pleased with the tentative agreement. While the matter was awaiting court action, Detwiler took his forces to a point six miles from town to grade back to El Paso. Another contractor had been awarded the remaining four-mile contract of the initial ten-mile segment.

By the end of the first month's work, grading was about complete and a few weeks later the Texas and Pacific began delivering ties and bridge timbers for the new road. By the end of October, the right of way problem was partly resolved so that, though a cloud hung over the project, grading could be continued across the disputed territory.

Rail from the east began to arrive over the T&P in November and soon the track layers were moving northeasterly in the shadow of Franklin Mountain. As darkness closed in on the last day of November, a small group of men watched the last rail being placed. Soon all the spikes were driven except four, and for this honor Colonel C. S. Masten, chief engineer of the KCEP&M, selected four men whose lives in the recent months had been heavily dedicated to the railroad, to finish the job. The honored gentlemen "performed in a tenderfoot style" to the amusement of the experienced track-laying forces.

An excursion was quickly organized and using the construction locomotive, borrowed from the T&P, flat cars and coaches (also borrowed), 200 people went out to the end of the line the next day. The starting point of the trip was near one street car line and the conductor entered into the spirit of the day when he told the excursionists as they were about to leave his car, "Change cars for White Oaks."

The excursion was a success, the company's wells at the end of the line were noted and the water tasted. A townsite had already been projected at this spot and Mrs. Magoffin suggested "Lanoria," taken from the Spanish, "La Noria," meaning "the well," which was adopted.

A second excursion was run a few days later and to the outsiders all looked well. The scenery to the north was capped by the snow-covered Organ Mountains, glistening "with rare beauty in the sunshine." Though only ten miles of tracks had been put down, grading was completed for the next 21 miles and the promise that trains would be in White Oaks a year later seemed entirely plausible.

Then it happened. The day after the second excursion three suits were filed against the railroad for unpaid bills aggregating $22,000, the largest portion being unpaid freight charges owed to the T&P.

"It is a temporary embarrassment," declared President Newman when questioned by the *El Paso Times*. While admitting that there would be some delay and annoyance, Newman felt that work would be resumed shortly and carried on to completion. However, that was not to be, optimistic statements notwithstanding. The financial support from New York dissolved, litigation ensued and the whole project became dormant.

Plagued by a three-year drought and then the depression of 1893, Locke wandered in and out of banks seeking aid but no funds were forthcoming. The KCEP&M was purchased by the Texas & Pacific in 1892 for $50,000 but on a closer examination they declined to revive the road.

Along the Pecos Valley in eastern New Mexico, Charles B. Eddy and J. J. Hagerman had been developing an irrigation and railroad project. Financial problems had confronted the two men with the result that they parted company. Eddy found the idea of a railroad from El Paso to Liberal, Kansas, to connect

Orogrande, New Mexico was the junction of the short branch to the mines at Jarilla. From 1913 to 1926, the Colorado Fuel & Iron Company shipped iron ore from its mines to the furnaces at Pueblo. It was also the first available water for steam locomotives north of El Paso, fifty miles away. Library of Congress.

with the Chicago, Rock Island and Pacific alluring and approached the management of that road. The hierarchy listened, then demurred. Undaunted, Eddy merely went elsewhere.

Things were improving in the business world and Eddy, with the bravado found in natural promoters, was soon knocking at the doors of other moneyed men. He drew sufficient interest from a group of Pennsylvania coal men to lure them out to New Mexico in the spring of 1897. Traveling by private car, the group then went on a camping trip in the area to be served by the Eddy railroad. The trip was well planned, the country was beautiful and the men were impressed sufficiently to back the new railroad.

For his own reasons, Mr. Eddy was not very communicative with the public or the press. With no word from him, there was little reason for El Paso people to anticipate another rail-

The early locomotives of the El Paso & Southwestern Railroad came through a number of ownerships with changing names and numbers. A characteristic of many EP&SW locomotives was the graceful curve at the top of the cab window. EP&SW 65 first bore the ownership markings of the EP&RI which were followed by EP&NE. It was later sold to the American Smelting and Refining Company for use in its mines in Mexico. H. L. Broadbelt Collection.

road. It was an unscheduled and surprise appearance of a group of men before the El Paso city fathers seeking a franchise that brought things out in the open. The only trouble was that William Burges and his associates who made the appearance were not there to promote the cause of Charles Eddy; they were there in the interests of their own line, the El Paso and White Oaks Railway, for which incorporation papers had been filed in Texas and New Mexico only a few days before.

Rising to the occasion, the Eddy forces rallied. Their attorney, the famed William Ashton Hawkins, strode into the city council to challenge the interlopers who by then all but had the franchise firmly clutched in their hands. They lost to Hawkins because of their inability (or unwillingness) to put up a $10,000 performance bond and the Eddy syndicate was saved. The El Paso and Northeastern Railroad Company was incorporated both in Texas and New Mexico (for the latter, the name was changed to use the word "Railway" in lieu of "Railroad") within a few weeks.

Charles B. Eddy was president of both companies while his brother, John A., was general manager. Having already spent

EP&NE 24 (top) *came from the New Mexico Railway and Coal Company and later became EP&SW 138. With 69-inch drivers, it was used in passenger service.* H. L. Broadbelt Collection.
EP&RI 58 was built by Baldwin in 1901. It was absorbed into the EP&SW roster as No. 190 and was one of the 19 locomotives sold to the AS&R in 1916, 1919, and 1920 for use in Mexico. H. L. Broadbelt Collection.

some weeks traveling up and down the route of their railroad to determine its final location, they were now ready to order rails, ties and equipment and let construction contracts. George S. Good & Company was awarded the contract for the first 85 miles (to what became Alamogordo) late in November 1897. Until wells were drilled—an old T&P water man, Mr. Gill, was hired for this purpose—the contractor faced the task of hauling water 50 miles. Ties were obtained from East Texas and locomotives from Baldwin. A batch of secondhand rails from an abandoned Texas coal railroad enabled Eddy's forces to have the first tracks down before the end of the year.

EP&SW 119 at El Paso shops in 1906. Formerly EP&NE 5, it was sold to the United Verde Extension Mining Company of Jerome in 1917. S. T. Borden Collection.

Eddy had purchased the old KCEP&M grade from the Texas & Pacific but only four miles was utilized in the construction near El Paso. With the terrain rising so easily into New Mexico as to give the impression of being almost level, the graders moved ahead rapidly, followed by the track layers.

Eighty-five miles from El Paso was the Oliver Lee ranch which Eddy had already purchased and, with the subdividing under way, the city of Alamogordo was born. In June 1898 there was a town lot sale and in the same month the first locomotive whistles, signaling instructions to the rear brakemen, brought a new kind of sound to the previously quiet land. Alamogordo for many years was the headquarters of the EP&NE with the offices, shops and a company hospital.

At Alamogordo, Eddy had a choice of places to build his next railroad segment which he resolved by doing both sections almost at once. The railroads were different from each other in almost every respect except the gauges which continued to

With switchbacks and 6.4% ruling grades, the Alamogordo and Sacramento Mountain Railway line to Cloudcroft and Russia is among the legendary railroads of the West. A large crowd stepped out of the flat-roofed passenger car of their special train to pose for the camera at the switchbacks. Completing the picture is the train with six cars of logs on the upper leg of the switchback. The locomotive is A&SM No. 102, one of four similar units built by Baldwin. **Museum of New Mexico Collection.**

follow the standard 4′8¹/₂″. The line going to the east was the Alamogordo and Sacramento Mountain Railway while the line to Carrizozo and then to Capitan (near White Oaks) was built under the same name as the section south of Alamogordo, the El Paso and Northeastern Railway.

The line of the Alamogordo and Sacramento Mountain Railway was probably one of the most spectacular among western railroads. To lay out the route and build it, Eddy enlisted the talents of his chief engineer, Horace A. Sumner, who had previously laid out railroads in the Colorado mountains. (After

A second picture was taken soon after the locomotive spotted the passenger car on one track and then climbed to an upper track. The railroad route can be traced by the three trestles. **Museum of New Mexico Collection.**

1902, he went back to Colorado to battle the mountains again, this time for the Moffat Road.)

Starting at Alamogordo with an elevation of 4,322', the A&SM passed such stations as La Luz, High Rolls and Toboggan before it came to Cloudcroft, the location of the hotel (el. 8,627') and went on to Cox Canyon and Russia (el. 9,069'). To accomplish this climb in 32 miles, a switchback was employed and ruling grades of 6.4% were necessary! It was completed to Toboggan in November 1898 and to Cox Canyon in May 1899, but further work was halted until 1903 when a four-mile extension to Russia was placed in service. The railroad tapped rich timber lands and soon the Alamogordo Lumber Company was in operation sawing lumber and building logging railroads. Much of

*With sharp curves, steep grades, and **S**-curved trestles, the 12 mile per hour speed limit is reasonable. EP&SW No. 183 gingerly heads down the mountain entrusted with a combination car and open-air car in its care. R. C. Brandt Collection.*

A mixed train paused on the Mexican Canyon trestle on its way to the Cloudcroft resort.

the initial cutting found its ways into ties and bridge timbers for Eddy's expanding railroad system. While timber was going out of the mountains, visitors were coming into the mountains on excursion trains from El Paso seeking relief from the summer heat which could be found at the Cloudcroft Lodge or private summer cabins.

Passenger excursions continued until 1930 and the line became a "freight only" operation in 1938. Switching to motor trucks, the lumber companies sealed the doom of the little branch which was abandoned in September 1947. Today the scenery is still spectacular, even if viewed from the highway, several of the trestles still remain and the whole story may be found in Dorothy Neal's delightful book, *The Cloud-Climbing Railroad.*

As the train eases around the curve to the Cloudcroft station, the station "Hotel" is only five minutes away. The flange rail, a safety measure on trestles, was installed on all major A&SM structures.

An excursion train is about to leave Alamogordo for the cool mountain resort at Cloudcroft. With three open-air cars and one combination coach, the helper locomotive by the water tank will provide assistance. **R. C. Brandt Collection.**

Work on the EP&NE paused at Alamogordo for a short while before graders and scrapers moved northward to Carrizozo, 57 miles, where the line turned abruptly eastward to Capitan and the Salado coal fields. The 21-mile extension to Capitan was opened September 29, 1899 and, from an operating viewpoint, this branch was only slightly less formidable than the Cloudcroft branch. The summit, Indian Divide, was surmounted by a ruling grade of 4.3% and a switchback. Although there were no special rules calling for the stopping and cooling of wheels (this had to be done at Pinto and La Luz on the Cloudcroft branch), rule No. 2 read: "Examine train and test air before leaving Indian Divide."

The great coal fields in the White Oaks region were disappointing but Eddy was ready for that eventuality and had already cast his sights elsewhere. Farther north were the coal

Capacity of Sidings in Car Lengths		SECOND CLASS 970 Freight Leave Mon. Wed. Fri.	Distance from San Francisco	STATIONS	Distance from Russia	THIRD CLASS 971 Freight Arrive Mon. Wed. Fri.
				EASTWARD ALAMOGORDO SUBDIVISION WESTWARD 5		
				Time Table No. 27 — December 15, 1940 — Cloudcroft Branch		
73 W 125 EBFWPK	Yard	7.35AM	1382.8	TO-R ALAMOGORDO	32.3	3.00PM
				1.4 (A.B.S.)		
	YP	7.40	1384.2	ALAMOGORDO JUNCTION	30.9	2.50
				4.6		
15	P	8.00	1388.8	LA LUZ	26.3	2.35
				3.7		
11		8.20	1392.5	EL VALLE	22.6	2.10
				2.9		
14		8.35	1395.1	PINTO	19.7	1.55
				3.2		
13	P	8.55	1398.6	HIGH ROLLS	16.5	1.35
				0.7		
9	P	9.00	1399.3	MOUNTAIN PARK	15.8	1.25
				1.6		
6	WP	9.10	1400.9	WOOTEN	14.2	1.15
				2.6		
8	YP	9.30	1403.9 / 1403.5	TOBOGGAN	11.6	1.00
				0.2		
			1403.7	SWITCHBACK (West End)	11.4	
				0.6		
			1404.3 / 1403.9	SWITCHBACK (East End)	10.8	
				4.4		
8	Yard WPY	10.15	1408.7	TO-R CLOUDCROFT	8.4	12.20
				0.7		
46	Spur	10.20	1409.4	HOTEL	5.7	12.05PM
				1.2		
10	Spur	10.30	1410.6	COX CANON	4.5	11.55AM
				2.7		
2			1413.3	HUDMANS	1.8	
				1.8		
20	Yard YP	10.55AM	1415.1	RUSSIA	0.0	11.30AM
		Arrive Mon. Wed. Fri.		(32.3)		Leave Mon. Wed. Fri.

(3.20) 9.69 .... Time Over District .... (3.30) 9.23

.... Average speed per hour ....

Rule 206 (A). Schedule of No. 971 may be assumed by crew arriving Russia on No. 970 without clearance.

(Operating timetable) *Three times weekly, the branch line went to Cloudcroft and Russia and returned to Alamogordo. The five miles between Tobaggan and Cloudcroft required 40 minutes to traverse because of the switchbacks. Back in 1921, there were two daily trains to Cloudcroft during the week and one on Sunday.*

fields in the former Maxwell Land Grant which now belonged to an old rancher named John Dawson. Litigation was then in progress challenging Dawson's title to these coal lands but Hawkins, Eddy's very capable attorney, reviewed the testimony presented in the case and was of the opinion that Dawson's title would hold up in court. That was all the encouragement that Eddy needed; Hawkins was soon on his way to secure an option on the property for his client. Dawson's title was upheld as predicted and Eddy exercised his option, much to the chagrin of other parties who quickly converged on Mr. Dawson once the verdict was announced.

Meanwhile Eddy, with an operating railroad extending some 150 miles north from El Paso, was able to rekindle the interest

The Pecos River bridge marked the westward end of Rock Island construction and the location of the last spike in 1901. The locomotive was formerly EP&SW 375 and was built by Alco (Schenectady) in 1918.

of the Rock Island to meet his railroad at Santa Rosa, an established town 128 miles north of Carrizozo near the Pecos River. To close this gap, Eddy formed another company in December 1900 with the name of El Paso and Rock Island Railway Company.

The original surveys called for the railroad to follow White Oaks Canyon in its northward course but right-of-way problems brought a change in plans; tracks were routed through Ancho Canyon, about a dozen miles to the west. It had been contemplated that the Rock Island and the EP&NE would meet about the first of December in 1901. However, as early fall came, the date was moved to December 23 which still allowed eight days to put on the finishing touches so that the entire "Arrow Route" could be placed in operation by the first of the year.

Santa Rosa station is just northeast of the Pecos River bridge. It was also a train-order station and a source of water.

To meet even this revised schedule, efforts had to be bent in every direction. Laborers of varied nationalities were recruited from outlying points, brought to El Paso every few days in lots of 15, 25 or even 65 men and then dispatched to the construction site. The A&SM open observation car, not in use in fall months, was pressed into service to take the men north. It appears that there was some problem of getting the men beyond the confines of El Paso and its bright lights, so precautions were taken. One afternoon in October 1901, for example, 31 Austrian and Swedish laborers arrived in El Paso via the T&P and were immediately taken to Fort Bliss for a good night's rest thus avoiding the necessity of searching for the group which would have been scattered all over town the next morning.

In spite of occasional shootings and a strike of boiler makers in the Carrizozo shops, "The Front" moved forward. On October 23, 1901, it moved 60 miles north of Carrizozo to a point which later became Torrance. In doing so, it marked the crossing of the summit on the main line at Corona (el. 6,724') which, were

At the end of a 132-mile branch from Tucumcari, Dawson supplied coal for many years to the Phelps Dodge copper smelters and to the nearby railroads for locomotive fuel. Along the branch, the mixed train stopped for meals at Roy (seen here in December 1947) and, after arriving at French, it was another 19 miles to Dawson.

At Dawson, the hand-operated "armstrong" turntable served the four-stall engine house. One stall was utilized as a garage by one of the crew. **Paul Henchy photograph, Roy D. Graves Collection.**

SP 3425, a coal-burning Baldwin 2-8-0 inherited from the EP&SW, is on the service track at Dawson. In the absence of a coaling tower, the track is lowered to enable yard men on adjoining gondolas to shovel coal into locomotive tenders. A. C. Phelps photograph, 1947.

A coal drag leaves Dawson behind SP 3160 around 1927. This locomotive was built at the Schenectady works in 1907 and was part of the EP&SW roster for almost two decades.

Although it was sunny and snowless when A. C. Phelps took the picture of the Dawson station the week before Christmas of 1947, the temperature was seven degrees below zero.

The Dawson Railway and its successors, the EP&SW and then the SP, crossed the Santa Fe at French by a heavy deck girder bridge on steel towers. As the same structure also crossed the Red River, the steel bridge was 472 feet in length. The SP and Santa Fe interchanged freight cars at French and, while the SP locomotive was switching cars, the "combine" waited at the station. A. C. Phelps photograph, 1947.

it not for the modest 1% grade prevailing in both directions over the El Paso–Santa Rosa line, probably would have been likened to the crossing of the "Great Divide."

As the year of 1902 began, rail laying on the EP&RI was advancing as many as three miles on some days and in spite of water problems, the superintendent of construction, A. S. Greig, said that he hoped to meet the Rock Island by January 31.

Toward the end of that month it had been bitterly cold in New Mexico but the last spike was driven at 9:30 AM on February 1, 1902. The crowd witnessing the formation of a new "transcontinental" railroad was not large but some interested people had come all the way from El Paso while others came from Alamogordo and Santa Rosa. Stepping out of his private car, *Paseo del Norte,* that morning and wearing a smile of satisfaction and relief, was Charles Eddy who had come with a party of friends and associates, including George S. Good, the contractor. El Paso had waited two decades for this railroad direct to Chicago and at last it was here.

The objective of cheap coal in good quantities suitable for domestic use and for coke for smelting was still beyond Eddy's immediate grasp but no time was lost initiating work on the 132-mile Dawson Railway. As planned, it was to stretch northwesterly from Tucumcari, 60 miles from Santa Rosa by the Rock Island, to the coal fields at Dawson. To speed the development of Dawson, a railroad construction camp was established at French, crossing of the Santa Fe was accomplished by a high bridge, and the contractor's forces worked in both directions. In November 1902, a 19-mile segment of the Dawson Railway was in operation under a timetable between French and Dawson. At the latter point a mixed train left each morning, stopped at the station of Vermejo (later Colfax) then went on to French to spend most of the day there (a track went down the canyon to permit an interchange of cars with the Santa Fe) and then return to Dawson late in the afternoon.

From French to the connection with the Rock Island the route was in doubt. In spite of the number of bridges necessary following the canyon of Atarque Creek, it was the best route but the owners of the Pablo Montoya Grant refused to grant a right of way. Plans were made to switch the connection east to

Logan, if condemnation proceedings had been unsuccessful. However, the courts found for the railroad and the Dawson Railway was built to Tucumcari, with operations commencing early in 1903. At the Dawson townsite, some buildings were already erected and coal production was being recorded. It was not until 1905 that the new owners greatly expanded production. One of their subsidiaries, the Stag Cañon Fuel Company, operated $3^{1}/_{2}$ miles of tracks at Dawson.

El Paso and Southwestern
Railroad Company

It was the initial success of the Copper Queen mine at Bisbee, Arizona, that sponsored a short railroad from which grew a system of over 1,200 miles in length and, had the plans of some of its people been carried out, it would have been considerably longer.

In some ways, its history in New Mexico parallels that of the SP. Most of the construction was accomplished over a short period of time and most of the lines were built to connect the copper mines in Arizona with El Paso and the outside world. It began as a modest 36-mile railroad from Fairbank to Bisbee, Arizona, built in the name of The Arizona and South Eastern Rail Road in 1888–89. Later there was an extension to Benson and another to Naco (both in Arizona) but the real expansion got under way in 1900 when the "Bisbee road," as it was called locally, began to build to the east.

Enlargement of the copper smelter could not be readily accomplished in the narrow canyon surrounding Bisbee, so a new site about 25 miles to the southeast was selected. Given the name of Douglas, honoring Dr. James Douglas, the man who had been guiding the destinies of the Copper Queen for a number of years, the new town began to grow with the arrival of the railroad early in 1901. But, as the railroad kept moving "The Front" east of Douglas, there was considerable speculation as to where it would all end. There were some reports with a ring of authenticity that Deming, New Mexico, was the objective, for here were two connecting railroads competing for his traffic—an important consideration to Dr. Douglas—yet the route

Stations along the 165 miles of the EP&SW in Southern New Mexico were relatively few as the population then, as today, was scarce in that area. Hachita was the junction of the A&NM Railway, and Hermanas, named for the Tres Hermanas Mountains nearby (Sp. Three sisters), was the connection for Deming. The architectural style of the stations incorporated a lower-pitched roof than the Southern Pacific for the boxlike structures.

described in the filing papers of the Southwestern Railroad of New Mexico spoke of building from the Arizona boundary to El Paso. Rumors had the projected road building to a number of other places incuding Silver City. As it turned out, the Bisbee road was to build to both Deming and El Paso.

While construction forces continued to work east from Douglas, another crew began grading south from Deming in June 1901 over almost level ground for 31 miles to what later became Hermanas. Historically, this was not the first railroad graded south from Deming for about a dozen years before, the Deming, Sierra Madre and Pacific Railroad had visions of building from Deming through Mexico to the Pacific Coast. A grade stretched out to the international boundary near Las Palomas to go no farther as the financial house of cards collapsed.

The Bisbee road was a different matter. With grading completed, rail laying began in the fall of 1901 and construction trains were soon operating south to Hermanas. There was a little problem of direct interchange at the north end of the track as the new road did not fully realize its objective which was to connect with two railroads. Connection with the Southern Pacific was easy but to reach the Santa Fe a crossing of the SP tracks had to be accomplished.

Construction of the new railroad was headed for a slow-down for lack of supplies. Actually 79 cars of supplies were on hand at Deming, having come in on the Santa Fe; it was just a matter of getting the cars to the new railroad. There were two ways to get those 79 cars transferred: pay the SP a $5.00 switching charge, a price considered exhorbitant in those days, or secure permission to build a crossing over the SP tracks, a privilege which had not been forthcoming. To discourage any possible overt action, SP stationed guards along its tracks in Deming.

Obviously, this presented a challenge to the Bisbee road which by now had taken on the new name of El Paso & Southwestern Railroad Company for the tracks in Arizona and which would include New Mexico in 1902. The man in charge of the construction forces at Deming was Bill Darbyshire, remembered for his crew-cut red hair as well as his ability to meet difficult situations. Late on the night of November 5, 1901, he dispatched a couple of his men to a point several miles west of the site of the proposed crossing of the SP at Deming. Acting as decoys, Darbyshire's men fired their guns and the SP guards reacted by running to the scene to investigate. By the time the guards had returned, the crossing had been installed and the needed 79 cars were safely on the EP&SW trackage. The controversy was finally settled in the courts and traffic flowed freely from the Santa Fe or SP to the EP&SW.

Trains over the EP&SW between Bisbee and Deming via Hermanas began operating in February 1902 while construction continued eastward from Hermanas. The railroad was built along this lonely land to the Rio Grande, often within sight of the Mexican border. Just before reaching the Rio Grande, there was the Bowen tunnel to be drilled. Work in El Paso was carried on in the name of El Paso Terminal Railroad Company and its trackage was conveyed to another affiliated company, The El Paso and Southwestern Railroad Company of Texas. Entry into that city was not without some difficulties in the acquisition of necessary right of way but the 93 miles of railroad from Hermanas were completed in November 1902 and scheduled operations began near the end of the following month.

Compared with the SPRR, the EP&SW main line in New Mexico crossed the Continental Divide at 4,739' (155 feet higher than SP) but conversely its grades were easier, the ruling grade not exceeding 1%.

With the completion of the railroad to El Paso, the EP&SW operated 291 miles to Benson as main line with another 40 miles of branches. The growing output of copper from Arizona mines caused the construction of larger smelters which in turn brought about an increased demand for coal and coke. The primary fuel source was coal from New Mexico, so when Charles B. Eddy approached Dr. Douglas as a prospective purchaser of his properties, he found a willing listener. Eddy's New Mexico Railway & Coal Company was the holding company, not only for the system of railroads reaching from El Paso to Dawson, but also for the coal properties. Eddy's railroad was none too prosperous; one of the disturbing features of its operation was the bad water. New locomotives, fresh from the builder, would make one round trip and then be sent to the shops to clean out the alkali and gypsum clogging the boiler tubes.

Negotiations proceeded smoothly between Eddy and Phelps Dodge (owner of the Copper Queen at Bisbee and the Detroit Copper Mines at Morenci, near Clifton, Arizona) until the matter of the price was mentioned. The figure suggested by Eddy shocked the Phelps Dodge interests, thus suspending further conversations. Some time went by when Eddy, still anxious to dispose of his property, brought the matter up again only to be told that Phelps Dodge was contemplating an alternative source of coal north of Gallup. Eddy sat quietly, listening to the explanation, and then blasted their solution with the advice that all was fine except that coal from the San Juan field would not coke. Challenged, Eddy replied that he suspected the reason for their indecision had been the contemplated use of coal from that source, so he had already arranged to have many samples tested. Further consideration on the part of Phelps Dodge resulted in an agreement being made transferring the Dawson coal properties and railroad to them as of July 1, 1905. Almost

Rodeo was the most westerly EP&SW station in New Mexico. When A. C. Phelps took this picture in September 1952, train no. 44, formerly the Californian, *was running about one hour late. The dispatcher ordered it to wait at Rodeo for the westbound* Golden State Limited *instead of Hachita, the usual meeting point.*

immediately coal facilities were expanded and new operating arrangements were made.

At Dawson, the new owners built coke ovens in long rows and trains bearing coal and coke went down to Tucumcari at which point Rock Island motive power hauled the cars the intervening 60 miles to Santa Rosa where their own railroad system moved them to El Paso and the smelters at Douglas. The performance of the Rock Island in the handling of these cars involved too many delays to suit Dr. Douglas and he was determined to do something about it. Attempts were made to buy or lease this part of the Rock Island but all proposals were turned down. So late in 1906, The Dawson, El Paso & Southwestern Railroad was incorporated to build almost due south from Roy to Corona via Las Vegas to form a shorter route under one management. Surveys were made, then the Rock Island capitulated and entered into a lease agreement for these 60 miles in May 1907.

*In 1952, when the Golden State Limited was powered by a diesel
locomotive of EMD manufacture to Hermanas, Douglas, and so
forth, steam locomotives were still pulling freight trains. The scene
is at Anapra, just west of El Paso, where the two lines are in close
proximity. Franklin Mountain is in the background.*

Columbus, three miles from the Mexican border, lost its obscurity in 1916 when Pancho Villa raided the town and left a number of casualties.

Little is known about the two roundhouses that once existed along this Eastern Division of the EP&SW. The Carrizozo brick roundhouse, having ended its useful days by 1930, was sold for an ignominious $100. Seventy miles to the north was Duran where a wood roundhouse was dismantled in 1921; at one time there were three engine districts in the 331 miles between El Paso and Tucumcari.

The EP&SW continued to build new lines, mostly near the western terminus. Tombstone, a famous old silver-lead mining town, celebrated the arrival of the EP&SW in 1903. In 1912, the main line was extended to Tucson. Later, James Douglas, a son of Dr. Douglas, acquired terminal properties in Los Angeles as part of the plan to build there. He also secured a right-of-way between Tucson and Phoenix and was largely instrumental in the subsequent decision made by the SP to build an alternate main line through the latter city.

At the east end, the EP&SW purchased about 10% of the preferred stock of the Rock Island Company (holding CRI&P

One of the more colorful railroads was the Arizona and New Mexico Railway, which began operations in the two territories in 1884 as a narrow-gauge line to serve the copper mines at Clifton and Morenci. Below Clifton, there are six tunnels. Posed for posterity is this train, but the identity of the riders is lost. R. H. Kindig Collection.

stocks, etc.) in 1910, an investment lost when the holding company went bankrupt some years later. Short branches were built in New Mexico, the affiliated Burro Mountain Railroad Company was built to Tyrone, and the Orogrande–Jarilla branch, originally constructed in 1899, was extended to Zora in 1916 to serve a mining development.

Leader in the fleet of passenger trains operating over the El Paso–Tucumcari route in conjunction with the Rock Island, was the *Golden State Limited*. Other name trains operating over the Golden State Route, as it was later known, were the *Californian, Apache, Imperial, Cherokee* and *Arizona Limted*. Often these were little more than changes in name; seldom were more than three daily trains operated over this line. (The last train was discontinued in February 1968.) West of El Paso, some trains used the North Line through Deming and Lordsburg while others ran over the South Line through Douglas.

Between Douglas and El Paso, there was little population to fill the local trains. Columbus, New Mexico, a quiet border settlement, had a burst of activity in May 1909 when the townsite was opened with an excursion from El Paso and a barbecue. Some who remained were there to witness the raid by the troops of Francisco (Pancho) Villa in March 1916 in which many buildings were burned and 16 people lost their lives. When the United States Army moved into the area under the command of General Pershing in an endeavor to capture Villa, the border towns along the EP&SW had a greater population than ever before or since.

The water problem along the Eastern Division of the EP&SW (lines northeast of El Paso) was solved by taking water from the mountains rather than from wells on the flat country which contained water heavily impregnated with alkali and gypsum. Not only was it a matter of engineering, it also involved legislation and litigation to make this program effective; in the latter areas, it was the lawyer William Ashton Hawkins who contributed much of his skill to make this possible. In 1908, the Bonito pipeline system was built from the Bonito River to Carrizozo and northward for 107 miles to Pastura. With the installation of the water system of pipelines and dams, replaced or enlarged from time to time over the next 40 years, dependable train operations could be realized. (This water system is

The SP's Rio Grande Division largely operated in New Mexico but included part of the line linking Douglas with Tucson. This caboose was a reminder for employees to work safely. A. C. Phelps photograph.

the subject of a book, *Captive Mountain Waters*, by Dorothy J. Neal.)

The Tyrone branch was the last major addition of the EP&SW except for the inclusion of another independent line gained through another merger. During 1921, the Arizona Copper Company, Limited, the Scottish company which had shared the development of the copper mines at Clifton and Morenci with a Phelps Dodge affiliate for almost 40 years, decided to sell its interest to the latter firm. As the EP&SW interests were in a large measure allied with Phelps Dodge, the Arizona and New Mexico Railroad, formerly a subsidiary of Arizona Copper, became part of the EP&SW on January 1, 1922. This company, with 111 miles of road, had its beginnings in 1883–84 when a narrow-gauge road was built from Lordsburg to Clifton. The New Mexico portion (29 miles) of this 70-mile narrow gauge was constructed under the name of the Clifton and Lordsburg Railway while the Arizona part was called Clifton and Southern Pacific Railway. Even before the road was finished, the two companies were combined to form the Arizona and New Mexico Railway Company.

R. H. Kindig was ready with his camera south of Alamogordo when No. 3811 came into view pulling a train of 101 cars. The year was 1940.

At the time the EP&SW was building across New Mexico, Dr. Douglas persuaded the management of the A&NM to extend their line to his railroad at Hachita, New Mexico. This took place in 1902 under the name of the Lordsburg and Hachita Railroad, a standard-gauge road, to match the A&NM tracks northwest of Lordsburg which had been widened the year before.

In 1911, the L&H was merged with its parent, the A&NM. Four years later, a branch was built from the west side of Lordsburg to the old mining camp of Shakespeare and to the 85 Mine at Valedon, a distance of 3.66 miles. While the Lordsburg-Hachita line was abandoned in 1933, the Shakespeare branch was operated intermittently until 1972 and the railroad grade can still be identified in Shakespeare, now an interesting and well cared for ghost town. Nearby, a mile-long, narrow-gauge railroad using a Plymouth gas engine was operated in the late 1920s by Anita Copper Co.

An AC-9 paused in Alamogordo in November 1940. The drivers were 63 inches in diameter and the locomotive was 79 feet long.

The very precipitous decline in the price of copper following World War I caused many mines to curtail their activities sharply and traffic on the EP&SW declined in sympathy. Men prominently identified with Phelps Dodge as officers or substantial investors of the copper company, also held similar positions in the railroad. When the fortunes of one industry declined, the companion industry also suffered. Diversification of personal investments was very much in order and a deal was made to sell the EP&SW system of railroads, by this time over 1,200 miles, to the Southern Pacific Company for some $64 million, payable in cash, stocks and bonds, effective at the close of October 31, 1924. Thereafter it was leased to and operated by the Southern Pacific Company as part of the Southern Pacific Lines.

Looking west from the First Street overpass at the joint SP-Rock Island yards. To the right are gondolas with coal from Dawson probably destined for Arizona copper smelters. It is probably winter as the stove in the caboose is warming the interior while beyond the station, an engine is switching a car. Today the scene is

*quite different as the high water tank (left) is gone along with
many buildings formerly around the station. With the absence of
the Dawson branch and the Rock Island connection to Amarillo,
there is no need for switching as the preponderance runs through
the terminal, stopping only long enough to change crews.*

Rock Island No. 402, with its classic EMD styling, stands at the servicing facility at the east end of the yard in March 1966. This series of EMD power handled such trains as the Golden State.

Tucumcari

Most points in New Mexico, if served by a railroad, never had more than a solitary carrier. The exceptions were such places as Lordsburg, Deming, Santa Fe, Raton and Tucumcari, which were tapped by as many as four lines.

Until the Rock Island arrived in 1901, Tucumcari was a small trading point for cattlemen. Originally named Six-Shooter Siding, the people chose to call their settlement Tucumcari, borrowing the name from a nearby mountain. The background of the name is speculative, but at least it had a more genteel sound.

With the El Paso & Southwestern entering from the southwest, the Chicago line of the Rock Island from the northeast, the Amarillo and Memphis route from the east, and the Dawson Railway from the north, a traveler had a choice of four directions when departing from Tucumcari. Today the city is served by the Southern Pacific and its subsidiary, the Cotton Belt, with through trains, so its importance as a rail community has diminished. However, U.S. Interstate Highway 40 passes close by and avails motorists a chance to pause for rest and refreshment in Tucumcari.

3

THE DENVER AND RIO GRANDE WESTERN RAILROAD COMPANY

The Denver and Rio Grande Western Railroad, an outgrowth of the Denver and Rio Grande Railway of 1870, is a vital part of one of the Central Transcontinental Routes across the country. Locally it serves Colorado and Utah; that it also served a portion of New Mexico is a fact lost on most people other than those living along this line or those aficionados specializing in narrow-gauge lore. Though the mileage operated in New Mexico in recent times measured only 99 miles, in earlier days the lines operated by the Rio Grande and its affiliates totaled 290 miles and, if the partly constructed lines in that state were included as well, the total might well approach 400 miles.

Though other major railroads have some narrow-gauge lines in their New Mexico history, the Rio Grande is the only one that has always been narrow gauge, with the one exception of the Farmington branch which at different times existed in both gauges. The nearest D&RGW trackage to New Mexico today is the Alamosa-Antonito branch.

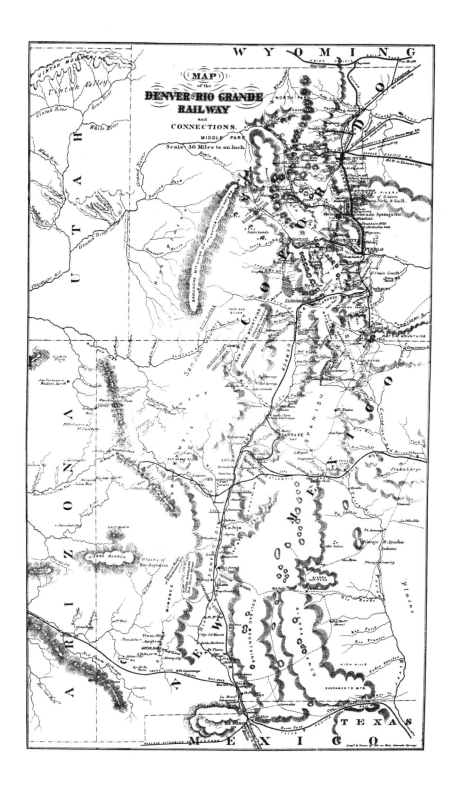

Having departed from the Union Station at Santa Fe, this mixed train is pointed north as it crosses the Santa Fe River. The site is near the Hilton Hotel parking lot. In the background is the San-tuario de Guadalupe, a former church. Otto C. Perry took this photograph in December 1937.

New Mexico had long been part of the Rio Grande plan for development for it would have been traversed in the course to Mexico. Losing out at Raton Pass in February 1878 brought about a change in plans and the D&RG decided to try another track. Previous to the hassle at Raton Pass, it had built westward from Walsenburg in southern Colorado and continued over La Veta Pass (el. 9,242'), across the San Luis Valley and arrived at Alamosa on the Rio Grande in June 1878. Meanwhile the D&RG was having its troubles under Santa Fe control which was finally terminated in court action in 1879. That year marked the beginning of two major branches, one going to Santa Fe, New Mexico, and the other to Durango, Colorado.

The 29 miles from Alamosa to Antonito were graded in the fall of 1879 and the following February track laying began.

The Rio Grande tracks occupied Guadalupe Street in Santa Fe.
The train is passing the Assembly of God Church. W. A. Pennington
photograph, Ted Wurm Collection.

Good progress was made on the line then destined to Albuquerque, though not as fast as anticipated as there was more
solid rock to be blasted than had been expected.

The AT&SF and the D&RG decided to bury the hatchet and
an agreement signed on March 28, 1880 limited the areas of
future construction for both parties for the ensuing ten years.
Under the terms of the contract, all D&RG work south of Española was discontinued, thus virtually abandoning some
$60,000 worth of grading in White Rock Cañon of the Rio Grande
and at Isleta Crossing. The line to Española was opened for
traffic on December 31, 1880, leaving a gap of about 35 miles
to reach Santa Fe.

The restrictive agreement, being public knowledge, invited
others to link the Territorial capital with the D&RG. For this
purpose a group organized the Texas, Santa Fe and Northern
Railroad in December 1880. The following October, a prospec-

The southbound train paused at Española station in August 1938 with No. 478 on the head end. **Richard B. Jackson photograph.**

tus in the form of a cheery letter addressed "To Investors" outlined the plans and prospective profits of the venture. Although the ultimate railroad was to extend from Santa Fe northwest to a connection with the Central Pacific in Utah on one hand and to some points on both the T&P and GH&SA (SP) in Texas on the other hand—in all totaling 1,258 miles—immediate plans were much more realistic.

Initially 37 miles of railroad was to be built between Santa Fe and Española (the distance differs according to source) which would constitute the San Juan Division. Estimated annual revenues, based on 30 passengers each way and a daily movement of five cars inbound and two cars outbound of freight, would provide $132,000. After all expenses and interest, $30,000 was to be left for the stockholders.

The second section of 38 miles was to go southeasterly from Santa Fe to Golden in the New Placers Mining District but only

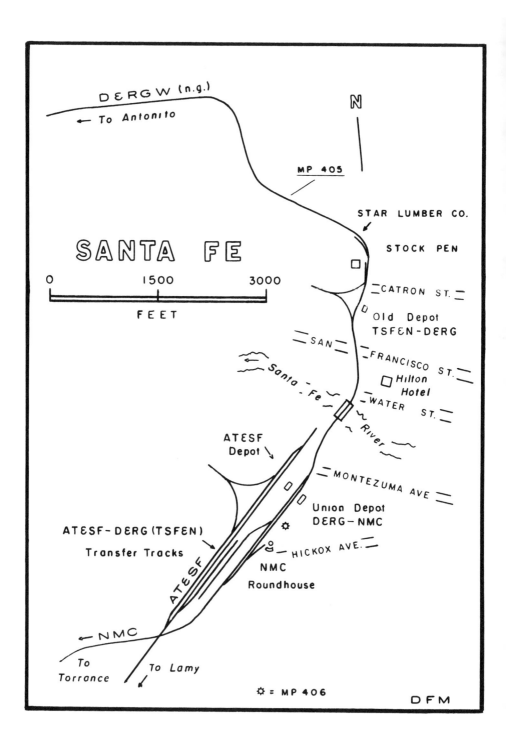

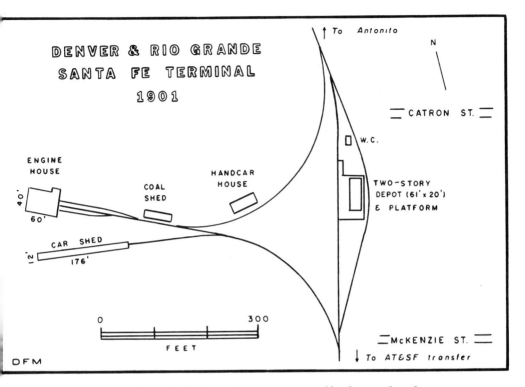

DENVER & RIO GRANDE
SANTA FE TERMINAL
1901

↑ To   Antonito

N

CATRON ST.

W.C.

ENGINE
HOUSE

40'

60'

COAL
SHED

HANDCAR
HOUSE

TWO-STORY
DEPOT (61' x 20')
& PLATFORM

CAR   SHED

12'

176'

0   300

FEET

McKENZIE ST.

DFM

↓ To ATSF transfer

Santa Fe, the capital of New Mexico, was served by three railroads for a quarter of a century. The AT&SF arrived in 1880, the Texas, Santa Fe and Northern, building north from Santa Fe, connected with the D&RG at Española in 1887. (In 1895, it became part of the D&RG.) Supplies used to build the TSF&N were delivered to Santa Fe, arriving on AT&SF tracks. The TSF&N built a 3,383-foot, narrow-gauge track, from the transfer platform with the AT&SF, to its own terminal.

The D&RG terminal underwent a number of changes after 1901. The three-stall engine house was replaced by two engine pits and the car shed and its lead track were removed. The coal shed was replaced by a shop building and an oil house was erected just southwest of the former coal shed. Just north of this terminal, the D&RG main line used a 110-foot frame trestle to cross Arroyo de Las Mascaras. The two-story station building also has vanished.

South of Embudo the tracks paralleled the Rio Grande. R. H. Kindig photograph.

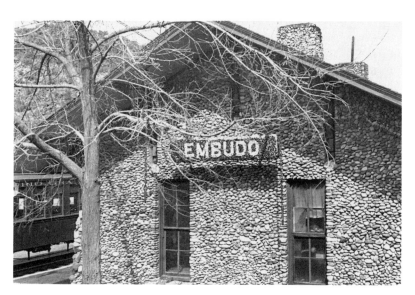

Embudo station, some 50 miles north of Santa Fe, was built with river stones. In the early 1920s, Embudo was a meal stop for train passengers. Jackson Thode photograph, 1940.

"No Agua" was both a descriptive and discouraging name for this station, 98 miles north of Santa Fe. However, according to a 1919 operating timetable, water was available for locomotives here. W. A. Pennington photograph, Ted Wurm Collection.

25 miles were to be built at this time to tap the anthracite coal fields near Cerrillos.

Work was underway the following year on this San Juan Division, grading was completed and much of the bridge work had been done before financial problems arose and everything came to a standstill.

The difficulties continued for several years and the prospects of taking the narrow gauge from Santa Fe to Denver, or any other place for that matter, appeared hopeless. Then, early in 1886, General L. M. Meily appeared on the scene to bring some order out of the financial chaos. With a new face at the helm, the citizens of Santa Fe took on renewed hopes and looked forward to riding the TSF&N. In August 1886, a commissary for the workers was established as part of the preparations for resumption of work. Ties were soon hauled to the grade and, with Martin Foody (later superintendent) in charge of the 60 graders repairing the old roadbed, real progress was evident. The first rails were laid at Santa Fe on October 21 and late Saturday night, January 8, 1887, General Meily drove the last spike at Española in four steady blows before a crowd of some 300 people. On Sunday the first passenger train carried

Crossing the boundary into New Mexico, this mixed train was en route to Santa Fe in August 1938. The tank bore the "Conoco" lettering. R. B. Jackson photograph.

These 25-ton box cars at Santa Fe were restricted to handling flour, sugar, and beans. D&RGW No. 3066 had been painted at the Alamoso shops just a few weeks before this 1939 photograph. Ted Wurm photograph.

A slow camera shutter creates the illusion of a fast moving D&RGW train north of Santa Fe. **Museum of New Mexico.**

200 happy excursionists westward from Santa Fe, then along the White Rock Cañon to the end of this line at Espanola where dinner was served at the railroad hotel.

Title to the property was transferred to The Santa Fe Southern Railway in 1889 and in turn, after litigation, was conveyed to The Rio Grande and Santa Fe Railroad in 1895 to become part of the D&RG.

Operations of the "Chili Line" as it was called (attributed to the dietary habits of its clientele) were casual. One left Denver on the overnight standard-gauge Pullman to Alamosa where transfer was made to the narrow-gauge coaches of the mixed train to arrive in Santa Fe's "Union Station" late in the afternoon.

For the engine crew, the run had to be made with cautious appreciation of the grades. There was a steady upward 1% grade from Alamosa to Volcano (el. 8,487′) where it reversed as the line went down slowly to Barranca. At this point entry was

In this classic well-identified photograph, one learns that the Santa Fe Southern No. 3 tried to cross a burned bridge north of Santa Fe in 1889 with mixed results. Some of the crew relax in the shade but some passengers were determined to be noticed. Arizona Historical Society Collection.

made into the canyon of the Rio Grande by a steep 4% grade with curves up to 22° for almost six miles. At the bottom of the grade was Embudo; at various times in the past it was a scheduled meal stop. Along the river the railroad followed a much less difficult course until it came to Buckman, 20 miles from Santa Fe, at which point the long climb (2%) out of the valley began, continuing to a crest near Santa Fe.

Branches along the line were few and far between. Between 1888 and 1892 a short branch was operated running west from two successive junctions near Tres Piedras, both confusingly called Stewart Junction. Each about two miles long, the lines were built to serve the Stewart Lumber Company.

Previously the D&RG had located a line in 1881 for 50 miles from a point probably near Chamita (near Española) in a northwesterly route along Chama River. Forty miles of grade were

As recently as 1940, the D&RGW narrow-gauge roster included 2,689 freight cars, 76 passenger-train cars and 56 locomotives operating over 741 miles of road of which 419 miles were south and west of Alamosa and Antonito. From Antonito, the railroad went south to Santa Fe and west to Durango and Farmington and substantial portions of both lines were in New Mexico. Four miles east of Chama was Lobato, named for a pioneer rancher where a train is crossing the viaduct. R. W. Richardson photograph.

When the last scheduled train to Santa Fe was operated August 30, 1941, D&RGW officials posed for this historic photograph in Antonito. Left to right: Claude B. Carpenter, Superintendent of Alamosa Division; R. Knox Bradford, Assistant General Manager; Edward A. West, General Manager; and Lyttleton F. Wilson, Assistant General Manager. J. C. Thode Collection.

Another view of the Lobato trestle. Heavy 4% grades necessitated helper locomotives even for short trains. With No. 497 on the front and No. 488 assisting, the "Cumbres turn" is negotiating the pass. C. W. Hauck photograph, 1963.

The Chama engine terminal maintained a coaling tower for the motive power based there. Extra locomotives were needed to assist trains over the stiff grades on the line to Durango. Many locomotives were outside-frame Mikados (2-8-2). C. W. Hauck photograph, 1948.

completed and ready for track laying when work was halted. Had this line been pushed on, it would have met the lumber lines running south from the Durango line.

In the spring of 1915, a large sign bearing the name "Taos Jct." appeared in place of "Caliente," which had been named for Ojo Caliente, the hot springs and town about a dozen miles to the southwest. A further change took place in the fall of 1915 when a new depot was constructed to replace the former box car used for station purposes.

Taos itself, famous for its multi-story pueblo, had been the objective of many railroad proposals, among them the Denver and Rio Grande which had done some grading in 1880 in an effort to include the old village on the main line to Española. Further surveys proved that such a route would have been impractical and Taos Junction, 20 miles to the west, was the closest that the D&RG came to Taos. Taos Junction was indeed a junction but the branch went west and north to La Madera. Built in 1914 to serve the Hallack & Howard Lumber Company's mill at La Madera, this 16-mile D&RG branch became a can-

A double-header, powered by Nos. 489 and 480, rattles across the Chama wye with a few loads of coal and a string of livestock cars. R. W. Richardson photograph, 1949.

A train of livestock cars is being switched at the loading chute at Chama. R. W. Richardson photograph, 1946.

At Monero, 19 miles west of Chama, D&RGW No. 486 is switching cars of coal in the fall of 1960. C. W. Hauck photograph.

didate for abandonment after 1927 when lumbering ceased. It was the declining traffic and particularly the washouts of the summer of 1930 that brought the matter to a head. Though the D&RG offered the line to anyone interested in continuing its operation, no one came forward and the tracks were removed in 1932.

The Santa Fe branch continued in operation until 1941 when, after the usual ICC hearings, abandonment was authorized. Local protestants expressed their objections to their representatives in Congress and for a while there was a flare of national publicity but this soon quieted to permit dismantling to move ahead and all the tracks were removed in 1942.

While the Santa Fe branch was under construction, the mining excitement in the San Juan Basin of southwestern Colorado

Dulce, ten miles west of Monero, had a touch of snow in 1954 before the train arrived. On the front are Nos. 487 and 492. R. W. Richardson photograph.

prompted the D&RG to push construction on another line, this one to go to Durango and Silverton, 216 miles from Antonito (245 miles from Alamosa). The initial 64 miles from Antonito to Chama were challenges to the surveyors and builders and later to the operating and maintenance men. To cross Cumbres Pass (el. 10,015′) a moderate 1.42% grade was laid out for the ascent from Antonito but, in the reverse direction, a 4% grade from Chama for 14 miles was necessary.

Crossing the Colorado–New Mexico line a number of times and passing through two tunnels, the railroad reached Chama, New Mexico, at the end of 1880 and service began to this point February 1, 1881. The narrow gauge continued in New Mexico for some 47 miles, crossing the Continental Divide, passing Monero and the coal mines, Lumberton and Dulce to re-enter Colorado, crossing the state line for the twelfth time. Following the San Juan River for some distance, passing Pagosa Junction (Gato), the railroad went over a divide to the watershed of Las

The **San Juan,** *a train of several coaches and an observation-parlor car, regularly paused for servicing at Chama, almost halfway between Alamosa and Durango.* **C. W. Hauck photograph, 1948.**

Animas River to Durango whose citizens greeted the first locomotive on July 27, 1881. The remaining 45 miles to Silverton were finished almost a year later as the usual winter snow caused suspension of work for several months.

Crossing Cumbres Pass, skirting along the cliffs of Toltec Gorge high above Rio Los Piños, made this one of the most spectacular trips on western railroads. Trains made regular stops at Toltec, New Mexico, to permit passengers to gaze into the chasm and to look with wonder at Eva Cliff, a thin and ragged pinnacle which some of the more adventurous men would climb to be rewarded by a splendid view. It was at this point that the members of the National Association of General Passenger and Ticket Agents held services on September 26, 1881 for President James A. Garfield who had died the week before. A stone monument marks the spot of these services.

The Denver and Rio Grande Railroad, long advertising itself as the "Scenic Line of the World," went on to promote an "Around the Circle Tour" which incorporated various segments of the

The Farmington branch had a checkered career. It began as a standard-gauge appendage to forestall the SP's ambitious plans to traverse the San Juan Basin but, after that threat passed, the branch was changed to narrow-gauge. The construction of a pipeline nearby in 1953 generated considerable traffic for this line. R. W. Richardson photograph.

D&RG, including the Alamosa-Durango line as well as the Rio Grande Southern Railroad. Starting out from Denver in either direction, one took the night sleeper to Alamosa or Montrose and transferred to narrow-gauge coaches the next day. Stopping at hotels in both Durango and Telluride, the trip was completed by spending the fourth night in a Pullman to return to Denver early the following morning.

A delightful narrow-gauge passenger train, in more recent history titled the *San Juan*, complete with a parlor-observation car, ran between Durango and Alamosa for many years. Unfortunately, even the summer patronage was light in the later years and the train made its last trip early in 1951.

There were a number of branch lines and connecting spurs, principally inspired by the lumber trade, spinning off at various

*Fred Jukes, one of the great legendary railroad photographers,
caught this double-header near Chama.* Colorado Railroad Museum Collection.

In 1938, the Texas Ranger, *starring Jack Oakie, Fred McMurray, and Jean Parker was filmed around Española. D&RGW No. 169 was temporarily modified for the motion picture.* Jackson Thode Collection.

points along the Alamosa-Durango trackage. Most important was the Farmington branch, extending 47 miles south from Carbon Junction (2.4 miles east of Durango) along the Animas River into New Mexico to Aztec and ending at Farmington, the center of an agricultural area known for its deciduous fruit.

There was an element of defense of its territory in the selection of the gauge for this branch; standard gauge was chosen when it was constructed in 1905. The Southern Pacific and, to a lesser extent, the EP&SW, were contemplating railroads into this area about this time. SP had surveyors working up and down the valleys to link the coal fields around Durango with Arizona and filed incorporation papers for several lines including "The Arizona and Colorado Railroad Company of New

Mexico" in October 1904.

A third rail from Carbon Junction permitted access of the standard gauge rolling stock into the Durango yards, a situation which prevailed for many years. Whether the wider gauge of the Farmington branch was the controlling reason that the A&C R.R. was not built is highly speculative but, from the Rio Grande viewpoint, the important thing was that it was not built. With the threat of a rival removed, the gauge of this branch was changed in 1923 to conform with the neighboring narrow gauge.

Little by little the narrow-gauge lines of the Rio Grande were widened, if traffic potential warranted, or abandoned so that with the widening of the Monarch branch in 1956, the only remaining narrow lines were the 264 miles of railroad west of Antonito, extending to Durango, Silverton and Farmington. (There was also 29 miles of third rail operation between Alamosa and Antonito.)

In September 1967, the D&RGW filed a petition with the ICC seeking to abandon the entire narrow gauge line from Antonito to Durango and Farmington. (The Silverton branch remains undisturbed.) Hearings were conducted by an ICC examiner along the affected segment of the railroad around the end of April 1968. The examiner recommended that abandonment be authorized, a view not acceptable to the many individuals whose interest in the narrow gauge transcended economic reality. The Commission concurred in the recommended abandonment during July 1969. That there were reasons to support the continuation of this line was evidenced by various alternate proposals, including the adoption of the remaining narrow gauge as a National Historic Site. In 1970, the states of Colorado and New Mexico, working together, developed a successful plan to save a portion of the former D&RGW narrow gauge. With much help from dedicated volunteers, the Cumbres and Toltec Scenic Railroad, extending from Chama, New Mexico, to Antonito, Colorado, a distance of 64 miles, was prepared for a revival, and the Railroad Club of New Mexico sponsored the first excursion on June 26, 1971. Since that date, this tourist railroad, operating from June to early October, has delighted many visitors. There have been several operators but the continued success of this little railroad, to a large measure, can be attributed to the volunteer workers.

Hoping to lure travelers over its new railroad, the Denver, Texas & Fort Worth Railroad issued a colorful timetable in 1889. The Bancroft Library.

THE COLORADO AND SOUTHERN RAILWAY COMPANY

One way to join Colorado and Texas by rail is through New Mexico and that is the route adopted by the builders of the Colorado and Southern Railway.

Two men holding important positions in western history, working from distant points, agreed to combine their efforts to link Denver with Fort Worth, 803 miles apart. From this linkage, a system of almost 2,000 miles in length developed. One builder was John Evans while the other was Grenville M. Dodge. Evans, a Chicago physician, went to Colorado to become its governor and to engage in various other activities, including railroad construction. One of the highest mountains in Colorado is named for him as is the city of Evanston, Illinois. Dodge, a Civil War general, subsequently served as chief engineer of the Union Pacific and later the Texas & Pacific.

Starting in Denver, Evans constructed the Denver and New Orleans Railroad to Pueblo in 1881–82. Financial difficulties set in, and the company was reorganized as The Denver, Texas and Gulf Railroad in 1886, again with John Evans as president.

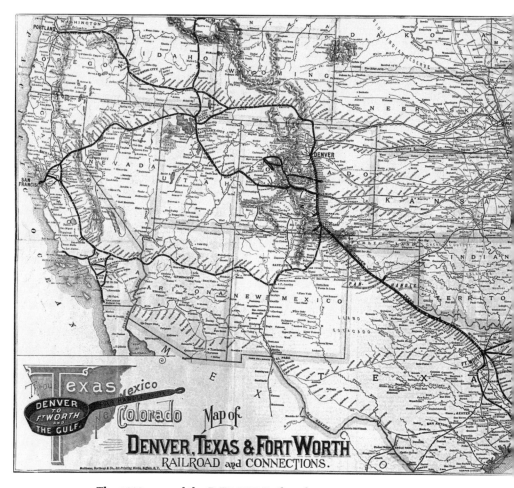

The 1889 map of the D.T.&F.W. Railroad.

The following spring, Evans formed another company to build south from Pueblo to Trinidad, Colorado, and through New Mexico to the Texas boundary under the name of The Denver, Texas and Fort Worth Railroad Company. Construction began shortly thereafter but by securing trackage rights over the Denver and Rio Grande from Pueblo to Trinidad, it was able to proceed with construction from the latter point almost immediately. True, there was the problem of a difference in gauges, but this was solved by laying a third rail on the D&RG's narrow-gauge tracks. (In 1895, a separate C&S line was completed from Walsenburg to Trinidad.)

At Staunton siding, between Clayton and Des Moines, the silhou-etted snowplow-flanger waits patiently for the winter blizzards to cover the land.

Meanwhile, General Dodge had been extending his line northwesterly from Fort Worth, Texas. During 1881–82, his Fort Worth and Denver City Railway reached Wichita Falls and, in keeping with his agreement to form a through line, Dodge continued northwesterly across the Texas Panhandle to the Texas–New Mexico border. Though the corporate responsibility of the FW&DC Railway stopped at the New Mexico line, Dodge's construction forces continued in New Mexico to join the men building southeasterly from Trinidad. On March 14, 1888, the last spike was driven a few miles north of Folsom, New Mexico, and the spot was christened "Union Park." The location of Union Park has been lost; even the colorful timetable issued the very next year failed to include the name.

When the Denver, Texas and Fort Worth Railway was consolidated with other lines to form the Union Pacific, Denver and Gulf Railway, control of the lines in Texas (FW&DC Railway) followed the merger. This new organization, formed in 1890, meant that the Union Pacific controlled the lines from

The Colorado and Southern's Gulf Coast Special *is behind No. 353, a Pacific type engine (4-6-2), running across a barren New Mexico prairie in 1939. "A lonely little train in a lonely country."* J. C. Thode photograph.

Wyoming to Texas, a situation which was terminated by the receivership of both railroads in 1893. The present company, The Colorado and Southern Railway Company, emerged in 1898, again in control of the Fort Worth and Denver City Railway. Since 1908, the Colorado and Southern (C&S) has been controlled by the Chicago, Burlington & Quincy Railroad and the boxed-in "Burlington Route" label found on its freight cars, locomotives and buildings is symbolic of the 74.7% stock ownership of the C&S held by the Burlington.

The Colorado and Southern operated only one branch in New Mexico. Dating back to the days of the DT&FW, the 14-mile branch was built from Trinidad, Colorado, to Sopris, thence up Long's Canyon in 1888, terminating at Maxwell, Colorado. In 1890, the managers of the Maxwell Land Grant, in a further

A year earlier, the same train happened to be powered by No. 501 from the stable of the Ft. Worth and Denver City Railway, the Texas affiliate of the C&S. R. H. Kindig photograph.

move to develop their resources, persuaded General Dodge to extend the Maxwell branch along Long's Canyon into New Mexico to Cemetery Canyon where it looped back to climb over the ridge to a point in the Canadian River basin which was given the name of Catskill. To meet the objective of the managers of the grant, the railroad was extended in both directions along the Canadian River from Catskill to serve the prospective lumber operators. Northwesterly, a 12-mile branch was built to Vasquez in 1890 while a nine-mile branch was built southeasterly to Dunn's and Newton between 1890 and 1897. In all, the C&S lines southwest of Trinidad totaled 48 miles of which about 30 miles were in New Mexico.

Although there were eleven sawmills on this branch, their operators were not as successful as expected and traffic failed to support the line. In 1902 and 1908 all but five miles of the

In New Mexico, Clayton is the largest town on the C&S Railway.

branch were abandoned and the remaining five miles, between
Trinidad, Jansen and Long's Junction, were taken up in 1940.
(Tracks of other railroads to Jansen were used by agreement
following this last abandonment.)

The main line, entering New Mexico from Colorado, did so
only after negotiating the several canyons of the Cimarron River
and its tributaries, a route that involved much curvature including several horseshoe curves. The crossing of the Cimarron
was made at Folsom, a cattle shipping point. Two miles north
of Des Moines (el. 6,621') is the highest point (el. 6,693') on
the entire main line between Denver and Dallas. South of Des
Moines the landscape becomes more moderate and less grading
was required for the railroad as it headed for Texas. In the late
spring, the country takes on a beautiful green but snow fences
and a pusher snowplow are terse reminders of the sometimes
rugged winters. In the early days of the railroad's history there
are records of trains blocked by snow for nearly two weeks.

Locally there were not enough people in Union County,
New Mexico, to support passenger service but through trains
obligingly stopped regularly at eight or ten stations along the
83 miles of C&S rails in New Mexico. In a gaudy public timetable of eyecatching hues of green and vermillion issued in

1889, the Denver, Texas & Fort Worth Railroad offered service "From the SUMMIT to the SEA" and urged the traveler to "bear in mind, for his own convenience" that the Texas Pan-Handle Route was "the only direct medium of transit between the gulf coast and the mountains" Trains 1 and 2, *Mail*, operated from Denver to Fort Worth. An "accommodation train" supplemented this service south of Trinidad but, in effect, the mail train was really very accommodating for it stopped at every station along the way to lengthen the scheduled journey to 36 hours. Improvements in service and limited stops cut the time down to 26 hours in the late 1920s and added the convenience of a through Pullman sleeper from Denver to New Orleans via Southern Pacific. Patterned after the other Burlington streamliners, the *Texas Zephyr*, placed in operation in 1940, cut the Denver–Fort Worth time to about 17 hours. Declining passenger traffic caused train discontinuances; September 11, 1967 was the date of the last scheduled C&S passenger train.

Today, the C&S serves New Mexico with one freight train each way, stopping at such places as Folsom, Des Moines or Clayton to pick up or set out cars. A nearby sawmill provides lumber traffic from Des Moines and volcanic cinders are shipped by the Twin Mountain Rock Company. Twin Mountain, a few miles north of Des Moines, which the C&S curves around to climb to the summit, was the scene of the last train robbery of the notorious "Black Jack" Ketchum before he was caught, tried and hung at Clayton in 1901. Clayton, with a population of 2,968 (1980), and Dalhart, Texas, are the largest cities between Trinidad and Amarillo. An important cattle shipping point, Clayton is also the county seat of Union County.

Welded rail was about to be installed at Naravisa, the most easterly station on the Rock Island in New Mexico, where a fast freight rushed by in June 1969.

CHICAGO, ROCK ISLAND
AND PACIFIC RAILROAD

Apopular geographic term in the corporate titles of many western railroads has been the word "Pacific," an objective of the visionary promoters seldom realized. One of these lines was the Rock Island. Dating back to 1847 in Illinois, the original company soon became the Chicago and Rock Island Rail Road Company and in 1866 it took on the full name of The Chicago, Rock Island and Pacific Railroad Company.

Reaching westward from Chicago, the Rock Island lines stretched across Illinois, Iowa, Missouri and Kansas to Colorado. Under the name of The Chicago, Kansas and Nebraska Railway, the Rock Island sent out two forks across Kansas in 1888, the first one halting at Liberal in the southwestern corner of the state to be followed by the second line continuing across Kansas into Colorado to terminate at Colorado Springs (Roswell). At this time the Kansas City, El Paso & Mexico Railway was full of great dreams which were to vanish into no more than ten miles of track near El Paso. There was some question about the newspaper report that the Rock Island would build its own line from Liberal, across the "neutral strip" (Oklahoma) to Tascosa, Texas, Fort Sumner and Lincoln, New Mexico, and El Paso, Texas. Would there be two railroads from the north, some people of that Texas city wondered. Lending credibility to the report were several factors. First of all a party of Rock Island engineers, with teams, tents and equipment, left Liberal on the afternoon of December 20, 1888 with El Paso as the stated objective of their survey. The previous year, by an Act of Congress, the Chicago, Kansas and Nebraska Railway was authorized to build across the "neutral strip" and to continue southwest by the most practicable route toward El Paso.

On the other hand, if one were to accept as gospel an 1887 map featuring the Maxwell Land Grant which appeared in the *Commercial and Financial Chronicle*, there were some interesting railroads projected across northern New Mexico on their way to California. The Rock Island survey crossed three existing railroads in that territory: the DT&FW (later called C&S) near Folsom, the Santa Fe at Pembroke (near French) and, after traversing the Maxwell ranch, the D&RG north of Caliente. Taos would have been on a transcontinental line had the Rock Island followed this survey instead of the one farther south.

But instead of two operating railroads stretching northeasterly from El Paso, there was none. The local line at El Paso was in deep financial trouble and the CK&N had to abandon all work for the same reason. Eventually the property of the CK&N and its Congressional franchises were passed to the parent company. For twelve years, no productive steps were taken by the Rock Island to close the gap between Liberal and El Paso, a distance of over 500 miles.

At the south end after several disappointments, something was being done about this gap. By the fall of 1899, Charles Eddy's El Paso & Northeastern had reached Carrizozo and Capitan, thus narrowing the gap by almost 150 miles. Negotiations with Eddy to bridge jointly the remaining 391 miles began about this time but it took well over a year to complete the surveys, make cost estimates and draw up the joint agreements before the decision was made. Finally, on December 7, 1900, the Rock Island Board of Directors authorized the construction and work began soon afterwards. By agreement, Santa Rosa, New Mexico, was to be the meeting place which meant that

Eddy was to build 128 miles and the Rock Island, probably because of its greater financial resources, would build 263 miles, or approximately two-thirds of the distance.

The 263 miles to Santa Rosa went over "an unchartered sea," according to one recollection, which went on to say that there were no places of habitation except Optima, Oklahoma, on the North Canadian (Beaver) River and the X.I.T. ranch headquarters at Middlewater, Texas.

Building this railroad was not without serious problems. Shortly after work began at Liberal early in 1901, smallpox broke out in the grading camps and moved westward along the route to reap a heavy toll of human lives. Those that escaped the dreaded pox had to contend with highway robbers and tough gamblers that followed the tent city of the construction forces. The camps were "shot up" every night, according to one description. Water was scarce along the way and to add to the general discomfort, there were scorpions, tarantulas and snakes. Once a train was stalled in a cut by a cluster of rattlesnakes who had been enjoying the sun-warmed rails. Not including those run over by the locomotives, the men killed 56 rattlesnakes at that one spot.

In spite of these obstacles, the work did move ahead and in about twelve months, 263 miles of railroad were built. Besides Marcus A. Low, the attorney who had overall responsibility for the project since 1887 when the CK&N was marching across Kansas, two remarkable operating men stand out. D. A. Robinson, the engineer of the locomotive on the track-laying outfit, was so devoted to his locomotive (No. 923, later changed to No. 623) that once he had left Liberal in February 1901 he never brought his locomotive back to the repair shop. Working the train during the day, Robinson kept the locomotive operating by tinkering with it at night. On Christmas Day 1901, Robinson brought the track-laying outfit into Santa Rosa, thus completing the task except for 3,000 feet to the meeting place with the EP&NE, but he was not ready to call it a day. Almost immediately, Robinson piloted No. 923 back to Dalhart with a string of cattle cars.

C. G. Stevenson, the conductor of the same train, assumed the responsibility of keeping some semblance of order at "The Front." His leadership qualities, backed by his large size and

The Chicago, Rock Island & Pacific, with the EP&SW System and Southern Pacific, formed the Golden State Route, a short line from Chicago to Southern California, which crossed the Rockies at the lowest altitude. The Rock Island, essentially a low-grade, prairie line, moved its traffic with big steam locomotives: 4-8-2s for passenger service; and 2-10-2s on freight trains.

Pictured is No. 3033 with 57 freight cars. Leaving the cars in the yard, a hostler shifts the Rock Island locomotive to the turntable and fills the tender with water for the return trip. Both photographs, Richard H. Kindig.

his diplomacy, served to keep the tough element somewhat in check and to keep the railroad moving forward.

Complying with the laws of Texas, a separate subsidiary, Chicago, Rock Island and Mexico Railway was the corporate vehicle under which the line through Dalhart was built. Later the property was transferred to The Chicago, Rock Island and Gulf Railway, the subsidiary which held title to all the Rock Island lines in Texas. This portion of the through line has the distinction of forming one of the longest tangents (straight track) in the United States, extending from Guymon, Oklahoma, to Dalhart, Texas, 72 miles.

The New Mexico segment of this line was built in the name of the Chicago, Rock Island and El Paso Railway.

As the Rock Island enters New Mexico near Naravisa (el. 4,183'), it marks the end of a long steady climb from Kansas, broken only by occasional dips into a valley to cross a river. From Naravisa, the road points down to cross the Canadian River just west of Logan. A short climb brings the tracks to Tucumcari, after which it crosses the divide to Santa Rosa on the east bank of the Pecos River. Long fills, ten to twelve feet high and stretching for a half mile or more, necessitated considerable grading in the undulating country of northeastern New Mexico.

Just beyond the station, about a quarter of a mile to the west, is the Pecos River where the Rock Island built a 310-foot steel bridge in advance of the track layers. Completed during 1901, it enabled the construction of the Rock Island to continue another 1,300 feet to the previously agreed meeting point to await Eddy's forces.

The last spike was driven on February 1, 1902 and train service began almost immediately even though there were no telegraph wires to dispatch train orders. With light traffic and moderate speeds, smoke signals during the day and headlights at night were sufficient indications to operate in that area until regular telegraph lines and later block signals were installed.

Tucumcari and Santa Rosa grew very rapidly. At the former, the population in the two months to February zoomed from zero to 400, and five saloons were flourishing. Two men were shot just before the railroad was completed but the report was that the wounds were not fatal. Sixty miles farther west at Santa

The Rock Island crossed the Canadian River on this handsome steel viaduct at Logan, 23 miles east of Tucumcari. Logan station (shown here in 1969), like so many others on this railroad, suffered from deferred maintenance.

Rosa, stone foundations were being laid for the station and the ten-stall roundhouse. Even before the last spike had been pounded home, Methodist Episcopal services were held one Sunday and the new Justice of the Peace took it upon himself to bring about a reform by fining five men $10 each for carrying concealed weapons.

Now that the line was open, the Rock Island busied itself with plans to promote the new route to California. A new train had to be named and a prize of $100 in gold was offered. The response was terrific; thousands of suggestions were made and the company publicized this interest by putting out a little booklet with the history of the naming of the *Golden State Limited* in which there was listed several hundred alternate names of merit. Not included was the name, "Santa Fe Overflow," the suggestion of the passenger traffic manager of the competing road. The *Golden State Limited* went into service in November 1902 as a winter season train; year-round operation did not begin until 1910 and continued until 1968. Year round service was provided by the *Chicago and Mexico Express* (westbound) and the *Chicago Express* (eastbound) carrying standard and tourist sleeping cars to and from California and stopping regularly by schedule or on flag every fifteen or twenty minutes at all stations west of Herington, Kansas.

About a mile east of the Tucumcari passenger station, another Rock Island line ran eastward through ranching country and trading centers such as San Jon on its way to Amarillo, Oklahoma City and Memphis. Prior to May 1902, when control passed to the Rock Island, the Choctaw, Oklahoma and Gulf Railroad was an independent line reaching west from Memphis through Oklahoma City and was nearing the Texas Panhandle. By the end of 1902, its Texas affiliate, Choctaw, Oklahoma and Texas Railroad had arrived at Amarillo. Some preliminary work had been done in New Mexico in 1903 on this line under the name of the Chicago, Rock Island and Choctaw Railway Company.

In July 1904, after 20 miles of grading had been done west of Amarillo, all work was suspended as the business outlook was unfavorable. No work was done for three years but in May 1908 rails were laid on the 20 miles of dormant railroad. In contrast with the line to Santa Rosa, work moved slowly and

The threatening storm near Adrian, Texas is an appropriate background for the demise of the Rock Island, once a great railroad. With No. 4422 on the point, two diesel units, six flat cars, seven boxcars, and a caboose, this was one of the last trains operated over this segment. **Don Hofsommer photograph, 1980.**

it was not until May 9, 1910 that the line from Memphis to Amarillo to Tucumcari was open for business. (The New Mexico portion was constructed under the name of the Tucumcari and Memphis Railway.)

With the completion of this last line, the Rock Island owned 153 miles of railroad in New Mexico. While surveys were run to the Pacific Coast at various times, the year 1910 marked the end of Rock Island's westward expansion.

In the late 1920s, new branches of different railroads were strung across West Texas and New Mexico. Dotted lines on the map of Rock Island passenger timetables for several years indicated two proposed lines in the Panhandle with one extending into New Mexico. From Vega, Texas, on the Amarillo line, the 76-mile branch was projected southwesterly through Deaf Smith County, then into New Mexico for 32 miles passing Hollene and terminating at Forrest, a town about 25 miles south of Tucumcari. It was the wheat fields that provided the impetus for this branch—5,474 cars of wheat were expected to be originated during the first year of operation. ICC approval came promptly in the spring of 1930 but an adverse wheat crop followed by financial problems caused the $2,289,137 expenditure for the branch to be postponed indefinitely and the branch was not built.

However, the asphalt sandstone deposits north of Santa Rosa prompted a highway contractor, New Mexico Construction Company, to build an eight-mile spur from Hawks northwest to the asphalt beds by the Pecos River. Over 150,000 tons of sandstone were quarried at this location during the 1930s and run through a small crushing mill. After treatment, the finished product was used for surfacing highways in that area and in adjoining states.

The gathering of the Kansas City line of the Rock Island into the SP fold has been reported on pages xviii and xix of this book. The Tucumcari-Memphis main line of the CRI&P has, except for short sections, faded into history and most of the rails have been removed. The last train from Amarillo to Tucumcari was operated on March 28, 1980.

The initial point of the Texas–New Mexico Railway began near Monahans, a station on the Texas & Pacific (Missouri Pacific photograph).

TEXAS–NEW MEXICO
RAILWAY

For a long period of time, the Texas and Pacific held the unfulfilled desire to operate a railroad in New Mexico. Several attempts were made, including the surveys across the territory to California and the subsequent purchase of the defunct Kansas City, El Paso and Mexico Railroad in 1892. It was not until 1930 with a subsidiary organized for this purpose that the T&P realized physical entry into New Mexico.

For decades, southeastern New Mexico, embracing Lea County, was an isolated stock-raising area. All that began to change with a series of events, the first being the drilling of the Hobbs Discovery Pool in 1927 which resulted in one of the richest oil strikes in the Permian Basin. The second event was the arrival of the Texas–New Mexico Railway in Lea County in 1930.

Formed early in 1928, the Texas–New Mexico was authorized by the ICC to build from a connection with the T&P at Monahans to the New Mexico line, subject to the adjustment of its route to include Wink, Texas, to satisfy local protests.

The station at Wink, Texas, was a modest structure in keeping with the community. It appears that most of the T–NM rolling stock was leased from its parent, Texas & Pacific, with one important exception when the reverse was the case. The T–NM purchased 200 hopper cars in 1953 which were numbered 100 to 299 and were leased to the Texas & Pacific. Fred M. Springer photographs, 1959 and 1958.

Construction began a mile west of the T&P station of Monahans (the T–NM operates over this section under trackage rights) late in 1928 and, by a three-mile branch from Wink Junction, the railroad was completed to Wink on March 1, 1929. Work on the main line through Kermit and the Winkler oil fields continued northwesterly to reach the boundary in June 1929, 34 miles from Monahans.

In December 1928, as construction was under way, an application was filed with the ICC to add another 71 miles to the T–NM passing through Jal, Hobbs to Lovington, all in New Mexico. By now the Lea County oil fields were attracting widespread attention and other railroads were considering entry into this previously isolated land.

Among them were the Missouri-Kansas-Texas Railroad, the St. Louis–San Francisco Railway and the South Plains & Santa Fe Railway, a subsidiary of the Santa Fe. The route of the South Plains & Santa Fe, the only one of the three filing an application with the ICC, consisted of a westward extension of its branch, which had reached Seagraves, Texas, in 1918, to Lovington, New Mexico, a distance of 46 miles. From this proposed line, a 43-mile branch was to go south passing west of Hobbs and Eunice and terminating near Henry. Hearings were held and the ICC granted the authority of the T–NM to build. Although the Santa Fe application was denied, the ICC felt that its line should soon be extended into Lea County but it was not built.

Construction was resumed by the T–NM in December 1929 after the favorable ICC decision and the road was completed to Hobbs in May and to Lovington on July 20, 1930. Though the railroad was not fully completed, the track was able to support the weight of a locomotive in time for a big celebration in Lovington a few weeks earlier. Acting as engineer, New Mexico's Governor Dillon brought the first locomotive into Lovington as a part of the festivities.

When the celebration was over, operation of the 111-mile railroad began. Tempted by the initials "T–NM," local wags came up with the nickname of "Toot and Never Move"—considered a mark of affection by the residents along the railroads in that part of the Permian Basin.

A train-load of coal from the Lee Ranch mine on the Baca Coal Spur with an electric generating plant in Arizona as its destination. Santa Fe Railway, 1985.

COAL RAILROADS IN
NEW MEXICO

T hough the presence of coal in New Mexico had long been recognized, production was only nominal, being restricted to immediate domestic use—until the railroads came. Not only did the railroads make markets hundreds of miles away economically feasible, their own hungry locomotives made them good customers of the coal mines. Before natural gas and oil swept away domestic heating markets in Kansas and Oklahoma and until diesel locomotives replaced steam power, coal was much in demand.

Measured by the states along the Appalachian Mountains, output of New Mexico mines was small but it was large enough to rank the state near the top of the western states. Annual production of coal in New Mexico crossed the 1,000,000-ton figure in 1899, rose to 4,000,000 tons in 1918, then slumped. By 1950, production was back to the 1899 level and then it declined further, eventually sinking to the 100,000-ton mark. The trend was reversed in 1960, reflecting the revival of coal mining at Koehler (near Raton) which the Kaiser Steel Corporation had begun two years earlier. Production today is prin-

Much coal from the Raton area in 1915 found its way into coke ovens such as these at Gardiner for Southwest copper smelters. John E. Southwell Collection.

cipally confined to mines near Gallup, Farmington and York Canyon for power plants and steel manufacture. Tonnage mined in 1968 was 3,400,000; by 1980 the production had increased six-fold to over twenty million tons.

Historically speaking, most of the coal has come from Colfax (Raton) and McKinley (Gallup) Counties, though such places as Carthage, Cerrillos, Hagan, White Oaks and Monero have contributed to the total output. The canyons around Raton marked the beginnings of coal mining as a major industry in New Mexico. In August 1880, Price and Stanley were supplying the Santa Fe with 25 tons daily from their mines near Otero and from a vein in Raton Canyon. Later in that year, the Raton Coal and Coke Company, jointly sponsored by the AT&SF and the Maxwell Land Grant Company, leased considerable acreage in Dillon Canyon from the latter company. A ready market

Blossburg had the reputation of being the oldest coal camp in the Southwest. This view is looking south. John E. Southwell Collection.

consumed the output for the Southern Pacific and Mexican Central; the Santa Fe used Raton coal in their locomotives. Two short Santa Fe branches ran up neighboring canyons to tap the mines. The first, built in 1882, began at Dillon, ran through Gardiner to Blossburg (extended in 1905 to Brilliant by the coal company) while the other, constructed in 1902, linked Van Houten (Willow Arroyo) with the main line at Hebron.

During the nineteenth century, McKinley County generally outranked Colfax County in the production of coal. The latter county had coal with a superior feature—it would coke—and from a series of events, coal production of Colfax County, running around 300,000 tons in 1902, increased ten-fold in the next dozen years. Significant events included the building of the Dawson Railway and the opening of the coal mines there in 1902 followed by the purchase of the property by Phelps

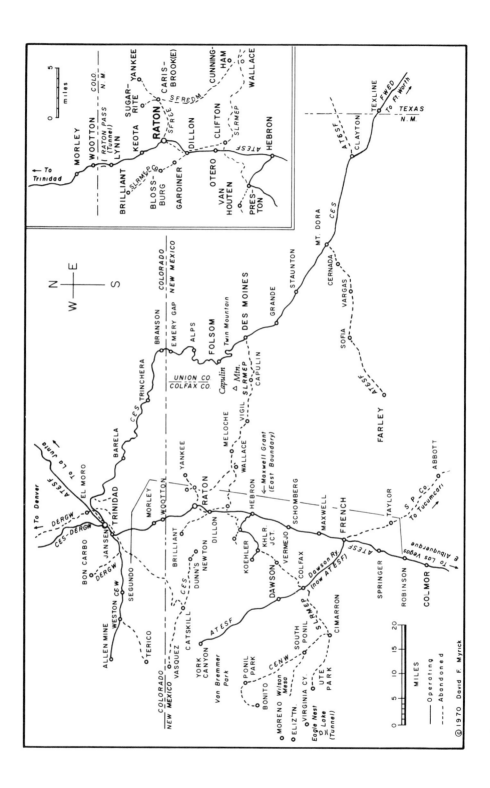

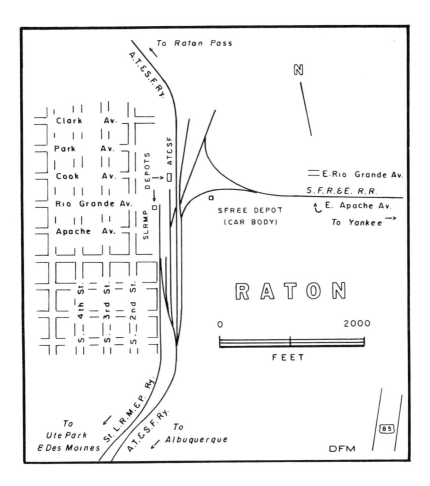

Dodge in 1905 and its subsequent expansion. Also contributing to the growing output was the acquisition of the Raton Coal and Coke properties by the St. Louis, Rocky Mountain and Pacific Company in July 1905 and the development of the smaller Yankee coal mines on the Johnson and Barela Mesas east of Raton.

Coke, in later years made only from Colfax County coal, was in great demand for smelting copper ore. For a time the upsurge in copper production necessitated the importation of coke from Colorado, Pennsylvania and even Australia and Germany and, to meet this need, many hundreds of coke ovens were built in New Mexico during 1906–8 bringing the total to 966, principally located at Koehler, Gardiner, Blossburg and Dawson.

Brilliant, in Dillon Canyon, the most northwesterly of the coal camps in the Raton area, was at the end of the railroad branch. U.S. Geological Survey.

St. Louis, Rocky Mountain and Pacific Railway Company

This railway was a subsidiary of the St. Louis, Rocky Mountain and Pacific Company which was formed by Hugo and Harry Koehler, St. Louis brewer and broker respectively, Jan van Houten, manager of the former coal company, and Charles and Frank Springer, both previously active in the affairs of the Maxwell Land Grant Company.

Surveys had been made previously on a number of occasions. When the Cimarron and Taos Valley Railroad was surveyed from Maxwell (on the AT&SF main line) all the way to Farmington in 1902, there was some talk that it would go to the Pacific and that construction was imminent. People, who were disappointed then when nothing happened, took heart in 1905 when the St. Louis, Rocky Mountain and Pacific Railway

The rails of the St. Louis, Rocky Mountain & Pacific Railway, also originated in Raton and headed south to Clifton where they extended in two directions: east to Des Moines; and west to Ute Park. A special event brought out this decorated train composed of three cabooses, a tank car, and the second-hand locomotive, No. 1.

let contracts to the Utah Construction Company and work was actually in progress that fall. By the summer of 1906, the rails linked Raton and Cimarron, almost 50 miles, crossing the Dawson Railway at Colfax station. The following year the branch to Koehler (coal mines) was added, the western terminus was moved a dozen miles to Ute Park and, by building the other way to Des Moines, a connection was made with the Colorado and Southern Railway.* Grades were not of great moment; the maximum on the Ute Park segment was 1.67% at the west end while there was a short stretch of 1.36% grade near Meloche on the line to Des Moines. On the latter line, traffic was so light that for years only tri-weekly service was provided but the coal, coke and lumber traffic on the Ute Park line supported daily mixed service.

Though a dotted line on maps projected the road into the Moreno Valley near the old placer gold camp of Elizabethtown

*The St. Louis, Rocky Mountain and Pacific Company built four miles of railroad in 1905 from the end of the Blossburg branch of the AT&SF to coal company's mines at Swastika and Brilliant. This track was then leased to the Santa Fe Railway, which purchased it in 1927.

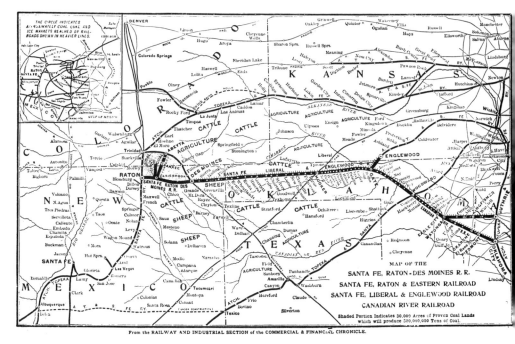

From the RAILWAY AND INDUSTRIAL SECTION of the COMMERCIAL & FINANCIAL CHRONICLE.

As indicated on the map, Raton was surrounded by coal mines served by independent railroads. The Santa Fe, Raton & Eastern Railroad was part of a projected system extending to Oklahoma City, according to the plans of the promoters. However, instead of 600 miles, the total operated never exceeded 20 miles.

Baldwin built five similar locomotives for the Rocky Mountain route in 1905–6. No. 101 was the first of the lot. It and No. 105 were sold to the Albuquerque & Cerrillos Coal Company of Madrid in 1940.

and then on to Taos, no substantial amount of work was recorded except a tunnel near Eagle Nest Lake. In 1907, the railroad reached its maximum of 105 miles. Some years later, when the editor of the *Taos Valley News* heard about another set of survey stakes near Taos, he observed that the rumor was unfounded and went on to remark that "If all the railroads which have been built on paper into Taos could be put end to end, we could travel from coast to coast without a stop."

Under the Swastika brand (an ancient Indian symbol), the company's coal was sold at retail and the railroad was known as the Swastika Route. After five years of operation, the owners decided that the combination of the railroad business and coal business was too much to handle (the cumulative net loss of the railroad during this time was over $1 million), so the railroad was sold to the Santa Fe on August 1, 1913. On March 10, 1915, the name was changed to the Rocky Mountain and Santa Fe Railway Company. Ownership of the coal properties was not disturbed.

The Santa Fe, Raton and Eastern Railroad

An independent group, headed by E. D. Shepard & Company of New York, had been actively promoting the Yankee Fuel Company, operating the Yankee coal mine, a few miles east of Raton. To serve this mine, the promoters built The Santa Fe, Raton and Eastern Railroad during 1905–6 from Raton to Yankee (7.4 miles) with a three-mile branch from Carrisbrook(e) to Lake Alice (cut back by one mile to the Sugarite coal mine in 1911). Although its roster listed only one locomotive, one box car, two passenger cars and 27 gondolas, it would have been the western part of a 597-mile railroad system if all had gone well.

Associated with this enterprise was the Santa Fe, Raton and Des Moines Railroad which built ten miles from Carrisbrook(e) to Cunningham (opposite Wallace). On the remaining 31 miles to Des Moines, generally paralleling the St. Louis, Rocky Mountain and Pacific, no rails were laid though the grading was completed and the trestles were installed. East of Des Moines,

No. 101, the solitary locomotive of the system, a 4-6-0 delivered by the Schenectady works in 1906, initially bore the lettering of the S. F., R. & D. M., which was subsequently changed to the S. F., R. & E. Charles Wingo, the fireman, was checking over the engine in 1918. John E. Southwell Collection.

The Santa Fe, Liberal and Englewood Railroad, an unrealized ambition, would have enabled the coal company to make direct delivery to Oklahoma City markets.

The whole system seemed doomed almost from the start. Total mileage operated was just under 20 miles. After the first year, the SFR&E lost money and in most years could not meet operating expenses. Regular operations of the Carrisbrook(e)-Wallace portion of the railroad (operated under contract) ceased about December 1912 and the floods of 1914 raised havoc with much of the roadbed. Financial difficulties brought about a reorganization of the railroad, coal, ice and water properties in 1911 as the New Mexico–Colorado Coal and Mining Company, which was soon followed by the New Mexico Coal Company.

By 1924, when the rail lines of The Santa Fe, Raton and

Eastern were sold to the Rocky Mountain and Santa Fe (an AT&SF subsidiary), only nine miles, from Raton to Yankee and Sugarite, were all that was left of the 597-mile dream. Raton was taking on a different appearance as the number of railroad depots shrunk from three to one.

The Santa Fe for many years has maintained its depot on the east side of South First Street near the intersection of Cook Avenue, where it is today. Also on South First Street, but at Rio Grande Avenue, a block to the south, was the station of the StLRM&P Railway, whose tracks followed South First Street and then generally paralleled the Santa Fe tracks to a point near Dillon, where an overhead crossing was made. The SFR&E commenced with a large curve from the AT&SF yards and ran east along East Apache Avenue. Located on this curve was the depot—a car body was utilized for this purpose.

Over the years coal mining around Raton diminished with the last operation, conducted by Kaiser Steel at Koehler, closing down in 1966. The Des Moines railroad branch was abandoned in 1935, the branches to Ute Park and Sugarite in 1942 so that now the Koehler branch was the only one remaining in the Raton area. One man, who worked for SFR&E in 1907–8, is probably the last remaining touch with that railroad. John Southwell, now 90, still engages in the mercantile business in Raton and has outlived the way of steel by almost three decades.

John Southwell is no longer with us and, on October 19, 1976, the last remnant of the StLRM&P Railway disappeared after the ICC authorized the abandonment of the Koehler branch. This branch ran from near Hebron to Koehler Junction and on to Koehler, a distance of 14.4 miles.

Dawson and York Canyon

Though coal mining activity in the immediate vicinity of Raton is now curtailed, it became very much alive in York Canyon, 25 miles due west of Raton. Increased demand for coal caused the Kaiser Steel Company to turn to York Canyon, in lieu of Koehler, where several hundred thousand acres of coal lands were acquired on the former Maxwell Land Grant in 1955. Preliminary surveys for a branch railroad were made by the

Dawson and nearby Loretto were towns in Vermejo River Canyon about 25 miles southwest of Raton where, under the name of the Stag Cañon Fuel Company, Phelps Dodge operated coal mines for over a half century. With tracks of the industrial and mining railroad everywhere and extensive plant facilities, Dawson was an important economic contributor to New Mexico. This view of Dawson in February 1921 is looking west; above the coke ovens is the amusement hall, or opera house.

Santa Fe as early as 1955 which were followed by additional surveys in 1961 and 1964.

The construction of the 37½-mile branch railroad from French to York Canyon at a cost of $4,000,000 was undertaken by the Santa Fe in May 1965. From French to Dawson, the abandoned grade of the former Dawson Railway was utilized but after Dawson a new grade had to be carved out of Vermejo Canyon. Twenty-three bridges, some approaching 300 feet in length, were part of the construction. Using welded rail, construction forces laid tracks to the mine site on November 19, 1965; five days later the first train arrived bringing mining machinery. The loop at the loading site was finished the following May and operating tests were made thereafter.

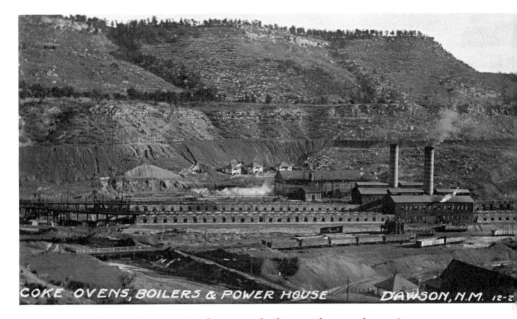

Stag Cañon Company's coke ovens, boilers, and power house in 1920.

No. 4 tipple and storage tanks at Dawson in December 1920.

York Canyon, northwest of Dawson, came into production in 1966. Coal loading was accomplished in a highly automated manner as unit trains moved slowly around a loop. **Both photographs, Santa Fe Railway.**

The job of the Santa Fe was to move 700,000 tons of coal annually over the 1,082 miles between York Canyon and Fontana, the location of the Kaiser Steel mill near Los Angeles. A unit-train concept was adopted; 85 specially built 100-ton gondolas could move a four-day supply of coal to Fontana. Beginning at York Canyon, the train moves slowly through the loading tunnel (two hours is required for loading), then heads for California. Ten to twelve hours is required for unloading and then the train returns to be loaded again. Test runs were made late in August 1966 and, on September 28, 1966, formal ceremonies were held to mark the first regular run of the longest unit-train operation over a single railroad. The Kaiser Steel mills in California closed in 1983, leading to periodic shutdowns of the York Canyon mine.

Madrid, contrary to its derelict buildings as shown here in 1969, was once an active coal producer with its own connecting railroad linking the mine to the Santa Fe at Los Cerrillos. For some time, the town has been a popular tourist attraction.

Cerrillos Coal Railroad Company

The coal mines at Madrid, northeast of Albuquerque, not only have the distinction of producing both anthracite and bituminous coal, but are perhaps the oldest coal mines in the West, said to date back to 1835. Commercial production began in the Waldo and Miller Gulches in 1888 but principal production came from Madrid, a short distance to the south. In 1892, the Cerrillos Coal Railroad Company constructed a standard-gauge railroad from Waldo, on the AT&SF, across the Galisteo River in the direction of the town of (Los) Cerrillos before turning south to Madrid, a distance of 6½ miles.

In 1901, the coal mines and the railroad were sold under

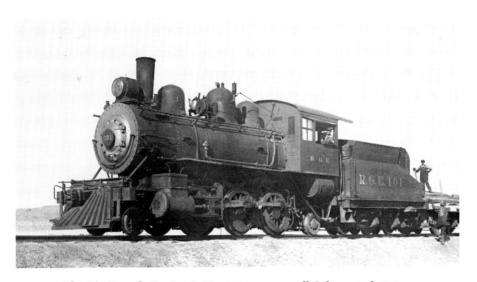

The Rio Grande Eastern's No. 101 was a small Schenectady 2-6-2 that first saw service on the spectacular Colorado Springs and Cripple Creek District line in Colorado. For some unexplained reason, almost every short line in Northern New Mexico had an engine numbered 101 at one time or another. G. M. Best photograph, 1933.

foreclosure to the Santa Fe. Production continued until 1954 when the mines were closed down although some shipments continued until 1959. The railroad was abandoned the following year. Madrid, no longer served by trains, has not forgotten the days of steam. Near the south end of a picturesque canyon is a museum with two locomotives (2-8-0). Formerly Santa Fe power, they were sold in 1940 to the Albuquerque and Cerrillos Coal Company, operator of the mines. (No. 769 is on display at Madrid, but No. 870 was sold to a southern California railroad museum in April 1989.)

The Rio Grande Eastern Railway Corporation

West of Madrid and 20 miles from Waldo was Hagan Junction, a point on the AT&SF main line from which the Rio Grande Eastern Railway Company began its course for 12.6 miles up a dry ravine to the Hagan Coal Mines, Incorporated. Initially planned as a private coal railroad, it was built about 1923–24, when it was decided to become an interstate carrier. Reincorporated in 1924 with a slight change of name, it commenced business to handle coal plus the products of a neighboring tile and brick plant. Traffic could hardly be described as booming; in 1930 two trains a week did all the work but there was a cooperative note that there would be "Additional train service when required." Matters, instead of improving, went from bad to worse as the mine was unprofitable and, after it was permanently closed, the railway, also a money loser, sought and obtained ICC permission to abandon its line in 1931 but continued to be operated intermittently as late as 1933.

The New Mexico Midland Railway Company

An inaccurate report of the coal mines was the reason for The New Mexico Midland Railway Company. The first coal mine at Carthage was opened in 1861 by Army troops camped in the area and for many years it was known as the Government Mine.

When the Santa Fe was building along the Rio Grande to Deming and El Paso in 1881, it added a ten-mile branch from San Antonio to Carthage in the spring of 1882. Coal was shipped from the mines until about 1895 when the disquieting report came forth that the mines had reached a point of exhaustion with the result that the Santa Fe abandoned this branch in 1896.

This seemingly well-authenticated report turned out to have little value for a good quantity of coal still remained. Under the name of the Carthage Fuel Company, coal was mined and shipped by wagon to the railroad at San Antonio. The high cost encouraged the construction of a railroad; accordingly the Carthage Fuel Company formed a subsidiary, The New Mexico Midland Railway Company in June 1904. Among the investors in this enterprise was Charles B. Eddy, previously president of the EP&NE and later vice president of the NMM Railway. Using the old Santa Fe grade, tracks were laid through the flat sagebrush country to Carthage where trains first arrived in the summer of 1906. Just before reaching Carthage, the railroad split into two lines, the main line continuing to Carthage and the Bernal mines while a mile-long spur ran in an easterly direction to the Hilton mine, once owned by A. H. "Gus" Hilton, a San Antonio businessman and the father of Conrad N. Hilton, a name familiar to hotel patrons the world over.

This railroad may hold some sort of a record for slow trains, if the schedules in the April 1915 *Official Guide* are credible. For the run from Carthage to San Antonio, one hour and 25 minutes was required for the ten miles and the return trip, being slightly uphill, necessitated an additional five minutes for its schedule.

This railroad was profitable and it boasted a handsome dividend record for a time. Unfortunately the mines of the Carthage Fuel Company became exhausted in December 1925 causing the railroad to limp along with operating losses until August 1931 when trains were halted. Formal abandonment was authorized by the ICC two years later.

Gallup Coal Spurs

Gallup is the center of the Gallup-Zuni coal field, which is part of the San Juan Basin coal area extending northward into Colorado. First production figures from the Gallup district reported 33,373 tons in 1882, most of which was consumed by the A&P Railroad. By 1886 Gallup was the largest producing area in New Mexico, a position it held for most years until 1903 when Colfax County took the lead.

From 1880 to 1925 many railroads were projected from Gallup north through the San Juan Basin to Farmington, New Mexico, Durango, Colorado and beyond. Both the SP and the EP&SW seriously contemplated such construction around 1905. Similar proposals continued after World War I; probably the greatest dream with the most unorthodox means of railroad financing was the Staley System of Electrified Railway. Its application to build was denied by the ICC in 1923 while the bid of The Colorado, Columbus & Mexican Railroad was turned down two years later.

The absence of a lengthy coal road from Gallup was, in

Gallup has long been the center of a coal district. The change in the size of operations is demonstrated by the loading facilities in the early days when coal was dumped into Santa Fe gondolas with wood sides and the more recent times when cars of a slowly moving train are loaded mechanically at the McKinley mine on a spur north of Gallup. **U.S. Geological Survey and Santa Fe Railway.**

some measure, compensated by the number of short spurs to coal mines. In 1920, a map indicated eight different spurs to coal mines reaching out from a nine-mile segment of the Santa Fe main line around Gallup. All but one ran to the north. The distance was usually only a mile or two, the longest being the two spurs tapping the Gallup American Coal Company, one to the Heaton mine and the other to the Navajo and Weaver mines.

The Gallup American Coal Company represented the continuation of a long tradition of coal mining. Formed about 1900, the American Fuel Company owned a 2.4-mile railroad from Gallup to Clarksville and related mines. Merged with the Victor Fuel Company (of Colorado) in 1909, it became the Victor American Fuel Company. In 1917 the latter company sold the New Mexico coal properties to the Gallup American Coal Com-

pany, a company affiliated with the Chino Copper Company.

Five miles west of Gallup was the Defiance Coal Company. A mile-long tramway carried the coal to the tipple of the abandoned Dilco mine which was served by a spur from the Santa Fe. One by one the spurs were dismantled as the mines played out or the markets diminished.

Despite railroad dieselization, New Mexico's coal industry has revived. The new coal market is fuel for steam plants generating electricity which, in some cases, are close to the coal mines but, in other situations, are quite distant from the fuel source. The latter situation has resulted in several new railroads in the Southwest.

Nine miles west of Gallup is Defiance station, named for a fort nearby, where the Santa Fe Railway opened the 13-mile

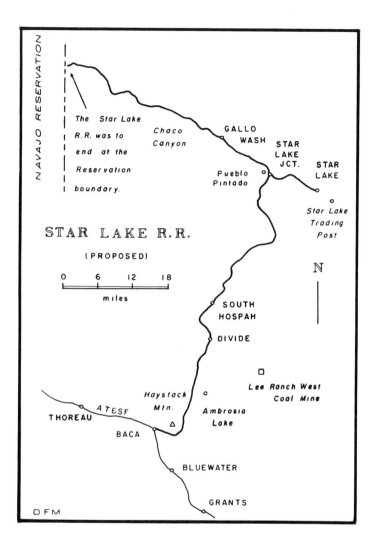

NAVAJO RESERVATION

The Star Lake
R.R. was to
end at the
Reservation
boundary.

Chaco
Canyon

GALLO
WASH

STAR
LAKE
JCT.

STAR
LAKE

Pueblo
Pintado

Star Lake
Trading
Post

STAR LAKE R.R.

(PROPOSED)

0   6   12   18

miles

N

SOUTH
HOSPAH

DIVIDE

Lee Ranch West
Coal Mine

Haystack
Mtn.

Ambrosia
Lake

ATESF

THOREAU

BACA

BLUEWATER

GRANTS

DFM

Defiance Coal Spur in June 1961. Originally built to serve the
McKinley strip mine of the Pittsburgh and Midway Coal Mining
Company, it was extended northward in 1974 for another eight
miles to the McKinley North Mine area.

A number of short appendages have been added to the Defiance Coal Spur in recent years. Navajo spurs, 1 and 2, were
built in 1963 and 1968 respectively and the two Erection Spurs
were constructed in 1974 and 1977. The Carbon Coal Company's loading loop, serving its Mentmore Mine, was opened
in March 1978.

Star Lake Railroad Company

In November 1976, the Star Lake Railroad Company, a subsidiary of the Santa Fe Railway, filed an application with the ICC to build a new railroad in New Mexico, 82 miles long. Starting at Baca (Prewitt) on the AT&SF main line, it was to run southeast for its initial few miles before turning northward to Star Lake Junction, a distance of 60 miles. A portion of this route would follow the crest of the Continental Divide. At the junction, one leg would head northwest to Gallo Wash while the other leg would turn in the opposite direction for Star Lake.

In April the next year, the railroad applied to the ICC for authority to build another 33 miles from Gallo Wash to De-na-zin Wash at the eastern boundary of the Navajo Indian Reservation.

Construction of the proposed railroad was delayed by countless regulatory problems and litigation. When those matters were finally resolved, coal market conditions had changed, so construction has been indefinitely deferred.

Baca Coal Spur

Although the Star Lake Railroad did not materialize, the need for coal to fire the steam boilers of electric generating plants continued unabated, so an alternate source was found. In 1982, a Santa Fe subsidiary announced plans to develop its Lee Ranch coal mines which included a 27-mile connecting railroad known as the Baca Coal Spur.

Railroad work began in 1983 at Baca (Prewitt) and was completed at the time the Lee Ranch coal mine began production in October 1984. The Baca Coal Spur, which ended at MP 27.3, continued for another 15 miles as the Lee Ranch Spur to end with a loading loop at the Lee Ranch Mine.

The route of the railroad, as constructed, differed from the Star Lake Railroad surveys for, after crossing the latter's survey at Divide, it turned east and southeast to the western section of the Lee Ranch Mine. Part of the mine output moves by unit coal trains under Santa Fe power from Lee Ranch to Baca and over the AT&SF main line to Navajo station in Arizona where

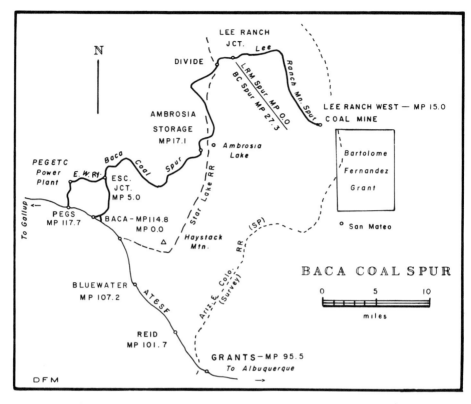

The crest of the Baca Coal Spur is at Mile Post 21.7 and is 7,431 feet above sea level. It is reached by a 1.74% grade eastbound and 1.50% westbound and is one of the highest points on the Santa Fe system.

a private railroad provides transportation to the generating plant of the Tucson Electric Power Company at Springerville, Arizona.

Escalante Western Railway

This railway, using the tracks of the Baca and Lee Ranch spurs and a small amount of its own trackage, is operated by the Western Fuels Associaton to supply coal from the Lee Ranch Mine to the generating plant of the Plains Electric Generation & Transmission Cooperative near Pegs, a point on the Santa Fe Railway, three miles west of Baca. The generating plant, three

The Escalante-Western Railway uses a substantial portion of the Baca Coal Spur to bring coal to its affiliated power plant at Pegs. Joseph P. Hereford, Jr. photograph, 1985.

miles north of Pegs, is linked by a spur ending in a loop constructed in 1980.

Initially, coal trains utilized a brief segment of the AT&SF main line between Baca and Pegs which necessitated careful dispatching and also required a use fee. This was avoided by building a 3.9-mile link in 1985 from the Pegs generating station to Escalante Jct. on the Baca spur, five miles north of Baca. The Escalante Western Railway brings coal from the mine to the generator over this trackage (41 miles total) four times a week. The roster of the EW Railway consists of three EMD locomotives (ex-C&O, rebuilt by Morrison-Knudsen) and 47 coal cars, including three spare cars.

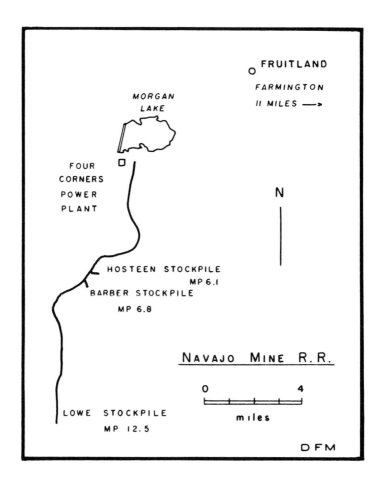

FRUITLAND

FARMINGTON

11 MILES ——→

MORGAN LAKE

FOUR CORNERS POWER PLANT

N

HOSTEEN STOCKPILE
MP 6.1

BARBER STOCKPILE
MP 6.8

NAVAJO MINE R.R.

0   4

miles

LOWE STOCKPILE
MP 12.5

D FM

Navajo Mine Railroad

On the Navajo Reservation, in the northwestern part of New Mexico, is the Four Corners Power Plant complex, which supplies electricity to several companies including Arizona Public Service, the manager of one coal-fired generating plant.

It began in 1953 when the Utah Construction & Mining Company (now BHP-Utah International Company) obtained a prospecting permit from the Navajo Tribe. After many steps in securing proper authority followed by construction, Utah Construction began deliveries of coal from its strip mines to the newly constructed Arizona Public Service power plant in January 1963. Both the plant and coal mines are southwest of Fruitland and, in the initial years, mining was conducted close enough to the power plant so that deliveries could be made by heavy-duty trucks.

As both the volume and length of haul increased, studies indicated that rail transport offered attractive economies, so a seven-mile, standard-gauge railroad was built. Opened in July 1974, the railroad was extended southward in 1983, lengthening the main line to 13.3 miles.

Railroad operations commenced with three Alco diesel locomotives and 22 Maxon belly-dump coal cars. As the nearest railroad was nearly 100 miles away, delivery of the locomotives from the railhead was made by low-bed trucks. With highway bridges unable to handle unusually heavy loads, the trip from Gallup was made over dirt roads often with a bulldozer leading the way, ready to widen or smooth the grade as needed.

The diesel locomotives had problems initially because the dust, resulting from the loading and dumping of the coal, clogged the oil bath filters. After obtaining improved filters, the problem was solved.

A review of train operations concluded that, because of the increasing tonnage handled and the then high cost of diesel fuel, electric locomotives could provide attractive economies. Overhead wires were installed, two General Electric 6000 HP locomotives, formerly used by Amtrak on the Northeast Corridor, were purchased, and electric operation of the Navajo Mine Railroad began in 1984. At that time, twenty additional hopper cars were purchased, which provides a shopping margin of six cars.

As now constituted, there are two unit trains, each consisting of 18 hopper cars with an electric locomotive powering the train. At the other end, is an idle diesel locomotive, locally called the "owl car," which is available for power in the event of an electric locomotive failure. While the cars of one train are being loaded with coal at the mine, the other train has taken its coal to the dump near the generating plant at the northern (opposite) end of the railroad where it is unloaded and returned empty to the loading area.

The single train operator manages the train by means of a portable radio control box. Taking his empty train to the mine

The Navajo Mine Railroad, near Fruitland, New Mexico, is powered by electric locomotives supplemented by diesel power. BHP-UTAH Minerals International, 1989.

for loading, the operator rides in the "owl" but guides the electric locomotive by his radio control. On arrival at the loading site, he steps off the train of empty cars, walks over to the other train, now loaded and ready, and, with the same portable radio control, he climbs into the cab of the electric locomotive and moves the train to the dump site.

Trains are operated constantly, three shifts a day, five days a week, unless demands for electricity are unusually high in which event the trains are operated six or seven days a week.

Tonnages of coal handled totaled 7.3 million short tons in 1988, matching the volume of some Class I railroads. The record handling for one day was on February 5, 1986 when 48,303 short tons were transported.

Local government on the Navajo Reservation is conducted by more than one hundred "chapters." Each coal hopper has the name of one Navajo chapter lettered on the side of the car.

Quirk (Uranium) Spur

Some more recent maps show a railroad leading north from Quirk, 32 miles east of Grants, to a mine five miles away. The mine is a uranium property of the Anaconda Company and the spur (built in 1954) enables Anaconda to ship ore to their mill at Bluewater, twelve miles west of Grants. The station was named for W. T. "Tom" Quirk, Assistant to the General Manager of the Santa Fe at Los Angeles, who died in 1945 at the age of 79. This spur was retired in 1981 although the track remains in place.

Very Large Array

One of the most unusual railroads anywhere forms part of the Very Large Array operated by the National Radio Astronomy Observatory. The double-track railroad of almost 38 miles interchanges with no other railroad because it has none of the usual traffic patterns and because the nearest possible connection is the Santa Fe, at Socorro, some 50 miles to the east.

The purpose of the railroad is to enable the movement of

Probably one of the most unusual railroads in New Mexico serves the antenna and transporter of the Very Large Array near Magdalena. Joseph P. Hereford, Jr. photograph, 1980.

an array of radio antennas into various locations with varying forms of positions or clusters for astronomical research studies. To locate the antennas in the desired locations and positions, the observatory uses "transporters" that are capable of moving along the dual tracks or on the ground. From a central point, the tracks extend in three directions, like the spokes of a wheel, for distances of eleven to thirteen miles.

The first segment of the Very Large Array Railroad was opened in 1973, and the completed project was dedicated on October 10, 1980. During the construction of this railroad, two 44-ton diesels were brought in by truck for use in ballast distribution.

RAILS TO THE
SOUTHWESTERN MINES

Much of the mining history of New Mexico is centered in the southwest corner of the state. Among the various mining communities in that area, Silver City, Pinos Altos, Tyrone, Santa Rita, Fierro and Lake Valley had railroad connections with the outside world.

Santa Rita

The copper mines at Santa Rita, now the property of the Phelps Dodge Company but for many years the Chino Mines Division of the Kennecott Copper Corporation, date back to almost 1800 when a Spanish colonel, José Manuel Carrasco, learned of the fabulous deposit. Production began in 1804, making Santa Rita one of the oldest copper mines in the United States. From that time to the present century, life at the mines made the full swing from great activity to a dormant state, depending on the Apaches and other factors.

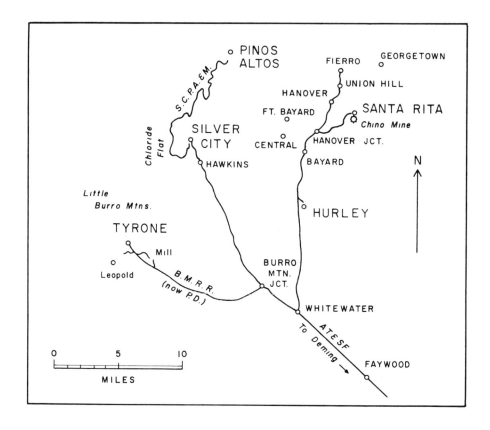

Shortly before the Santa Rita Mining Company was formed by New York men about 1899, efforts were made to connect the mines by rail with the outside world. There was already the Santa Fe branch from Deming to Silver City so in 1891 an independent group opened a 14-mile railroad under the name of the Silver City and Northern Rail Road Company from Whitewater through Hurley to San Jose, a station just east of Hanover Junction of today. Six years later this short line was taken over by the Santa Fe and in 1898, the Santa Fe extended the branch another four miles to Santa Rita under the name of The Santa Rita Railroad Company.

The big change came in 1909 when the Santa Rita Mining Company was sold to the Chino Copper Company. The latter company, blessed with strong financial resources, made the purchase after large reserves of copper ore suitable for open pit mining had been firmly established.

Santa Rita was the settlement adjoining the big Chino copper mine. AT&SF engine No. 366 has just arrived at the station with a mixed train. John G. Harlan Collection, c. 1920.

Work on the open pit began in 1910 by the Chino Copper Company, with side dump cars taking out copper ore and waste rock. Those cars with ore were delivered to the Santa Fe interchange at Santa Rita for the line haul of nine miles to the concentrator at Hurley (unless they were to go to the ore dump). The cars with waste rock were sent to the waste dump. In the early days, motive power for the Chino mines consisted of 21 0-4-0T locomotives of H. K. Porter manufacture with seven weighing 50 tons and the remaining 14 weighing 45$^{1}/_{2}$ tons. Not all of the 21 locomotives were expected to be in service at one time. In 1914, according to one observer, two were generally in the shop and another was "held just outside the shop with steam up ready for instant service."

Mine trackage, which began with a few miles in 1910, grew to 14 miles in 1912 and with subsequent additions, the spur to the northwest ore body built early in the summer of 1914

Bayard was a station on the Santa Rita branch. J. Lawson took this photograph in 1955. W. C. Whittaker Collection.

being an example, total trackage soon measured 24 miles.

The very nature of the mining operation, necessitating the expansion of the pit by cutting away the benches serving as the railroad grade, caused a constant shifting and realignment of tracks. As early as 1914 there were four track gangs each of 14 men assigned to this work. For track work on the waste and ore dumps, the same situation prevailed except that even more men were required, the gangs numbering seven again each with a complement of 14 men.

In later years, Alco and Baldwin supplied the steam power but in 1939, the first steps toward electrification of the pit haulage began with the purchase of seven electric locomotives from General Electric. Electrification of the pit haulage was completed two years later.

As the pit became larger and deeper—by 1963 it was over a mile wide in any direction and 1000 feet deep with 21 bench levels—it became more expensive to remove ore and waste from the pit. Truck operations were instituted in 1952 as a supplement to the pit railroad and efforts were made to speed up train movements and reduce costs. Centralized traffic control was installed for all switches in the pit. Rails in the main

As excavations went deeper and formed the Chino Pit, local rail-roads served the mine. Steam shovels loaded the dump cars with copper ore. Then the trains were pulled to the crest of the pit by tank locomotives, such as Kennecott No. 25, a 0-6-0T built by Alco in 1920. D. S. Richter photograph.

A view of the Kennecott reduction works at Hurley, eight miles from the Chino mine. Copper ore was delivered to the concentrator (above and to the right of the trestle) by cars from the mine. After initial processing, the concentrates were conveyed to the smelter in the background. Kennecott Copper Corporation, c. 1968.

By 1959, the shovels and ore trains were electrically operated. A cleaner operation was one of the benefits. **Kennecott Copper Corporation.**

tracks, formerly 90 lb. rail (initially 60 lb. rail was used), were replaced with 132 lb. rails. Track repair forces began using powered ballast tampers, track liners, spike pullers, etc. Other procedures were revised.

Still costs continued to climb. A skip hoist, completed in 1962, reduced haulage costs from lower levels by 37%. More trucks were purchased and, after careful studies, it was decided to convert the entire Chino pit from rail to truck haulage, with the last ore move from the pit by train taking place on September 5, 1963.

Today the railroad at Santa Rita is less than five miles in length. Operated in two sections by electric locomotives, one segment moves the cars from the ore bin, fed by the skip hoist at the top of the pit, to the interchange with the Santa Fe while the other performs a similar service for the ore delivered from the pit by truck. From the interchange at Santa Rita, the Santa Fe assembles trains of 50 cars for the haul to Hurley, dumping the ore into the bins of the primary crusher at the concentrator at Hurley. Since 1939, when the smelter was built at Hurley, outbound traffic handled by the Santa Fe is in the form of copper anodes for the refinery.

Fierro-Hanover

Besides having developed the Denver and Rio Grande Railroad, General William J. Palmer also served as the first president of the Colorado Fuel and Iron Company (now CF&I Steel Corporation). Sources of coal and iron ore are located in Colorado, Wyoming and New Mexico. For some years CF&I drew on coal mines near Gallup for fuel and from Fierro they took iron ore for their steel mills at Pueblo, Colorado.

Just west of Santa Rita is the canyon of Hanover Creek and in 1899 the Santa Fe built a six-mile branch from Hanover Junction to Hanover, Union Hill and Fierro under the name of the Hanover Railroad Company. For many years, CF&I quarried iron ore from the '86 and Jim Fair mines (opened 1899), Union Hill (opened 1901) and later from the Snowflake and Cupola mines, shipping it over the Santa Fe to Pueblo, a distance of almost 700 miles. At times shipments ran ten cars a day over extended periods. CF&I ceased operations at Fierro in 1924, switching to iron mines near Silver City for a few years. Small operators around both places produced and shipped iron ore to Pueblo for several decades.

Copper and zinc are also found in this canyon. The Empire zinc mines have long been an important source of this metal, the property now being operated by The New Jersey Zinc Company which also has similar mines at Magdalena. In 1966 when the U.S. Smelting, Refining and Mining Company turned to copper mining in that canyon, the Santa Fe extended its industrial tracks to serve the plant of the former's Continental mine.

Silver City

Dating back to the discoveries of ore by prospectors in 1871, Silver City has been an important mining town and was one of the first communities in New Mexico to be tapped by an independent short line railroad.

The time was March 1882. A year before the Santa Fe and the Southern Pacific had joined their tracks at Deming; now men from Silver City and elsewhere (including J. Parker Whitney of Boston who had bought the Santa Rita copper mines) incorporated the Silver City, Deming and Pacific Railroad Company. Work soon got under way on the 47-mile railroad and, even with delays, good progress had been made by the end of the year. In March 1883, rail laying had begun on this narrow-gauge railroad, trains were operating to Whitewater in April and, on May 12, 1883, Silver City celebrated the completion of the little railroad. Using railroad ties, two stands were assembled at Silver City, one for the band and the other for prominent speakers and guests. The assemblage was watching the track layers spiking down the last rails when work came to a halt. Mr. Scott, a member of the construction force, spoke up to say that he needed one more spike to complete the work. At that moment, M. W. Bremen, an important mining man, stepped forward, fished a silver spike from his pocket and gave it to the railroad men. Once the silver spike was positioned, Mayor Black tapped it in place. Adding to the excitement was the arrival of the first train with engine No. 1, which bore the name "E. G. Shields" honoring the road's chief engineer.

Even before this narrow gauge reached Silver City, the company had men surveying westward to Clifton. Previously, Col. Whitney had talked of another line extending in the opposite direction to Hanover, Santa Rita, and down the Mimbres Valley near the silver mining town of Georgetown before turning northward to the timber country.

Had the proposed lines been built, Silver City would have been something of a railroad center but, like so many railroad dreams of the last century, nothing materialized in either direction. Less than a year after the line was opened it was sold to the Santa Fe, but Whitney continued to maintain his interest in the copper mines for some years. Expectations were that the

The Santa Fe, running northwesterly from Deming, first tapped Silver City and then other points in this mineralized area. Sometimes things did not go smoothly. This mixed train had trouble in March 1897 in trying to negotiate a curve by Chinese Gardens, just south of Silver City. The locomotive and the express car remained upright but the box cars did not. John G. Harlan Collection.

Santa Fe would widen the 36″ gauge to standard and this was done on May 16, 1886. Some of the narrow gauge side tracks, however, remained unchanged for two more years. Several branches and connecting railroads were built from the Silver City branch and today it forms an important part of the transportation network of the copper industry. Changing conditions in Silver City in recent years reduced the tonnage handled by the portion of the line from Burro Mountain Junction to Silver City, a distance of 12.6 miles, and this section was abandoned on March 16, 1983.

Pinos Altos

The discovery of placer gold in 1859–60 marked the beginnings of Pinos Altos. Located about seven miles north of Silver City, the town was without railroad connections until the twentieth century. When the railroad came, it was there for only a short while and its gauge was only 24 inches, about two-thirds the width of the usual narrow gauge.

Mining activity, as it did so often in the history of western camps, had the customary vicissitudes at Pinos Altos. Typically, mining railroads were promoted either to lift the town or an industry from a dull economy or to take advantage of a boom. One group tried its hand promoting a railroad in the spring of 1888 connecting Pinos Altos with Silver City, but soon discarded its plans. Another group of local residents filed incorporation papers in August 1889 for the Silver City, Pinos Altos and Mogollon Railroad Company. Not only was it projected to Pinos Altos, but it was to continue for 120 miles northwesterly to Alma and Cooney in a silver mining area of the Mogollon Mountains. Branches were also proposed to Santa Rita and Hanover.

Though some grading was undertaken after the difficulties of obtaining financing had been resolved, interest in the railroad lagged and all work was abandoned. The mines at Pinos Altos and the smelter at Silver City, which had belonged to the estate of Senator Hearst, were sold to the Comanche Mining and Smelting Company in 1903. The new company, backed by Milwaukee, Wisconsin, men, went ahead with its plans on several fronts. In April 1905, people in both Silver City and Pinos Altos were delighted with the announcement from the general manager, C. J. Laughren, that the narrow gauge railroad would be built to Pinos Altos and that the smelter at Silver City would be repaired and enlarged to 400 tons capacity.

After acquiring the franchise and property of the old SCPA&M Railroad, a new survey confirmed the advisability of using most of the old grade. From the Gilpin Tramway near Denver (also 24-inch gauge), two second-hand Shay locomotives were purchased, delivery being made in May 1905. Already 50 graders were at work, ties were being received and progress was being recorded. Though the destinationof the 24-inch narrow gauge

The "Horseshoe Curve" and the "Hairpin Loop" of the Silver City, Pinos Altos & Mogollon Railroad were photographers' delights. This two-foot gauge railroad was powered by Shay locomotives including two from the Gilpin Tram of Central City, Colorado. Somewhere along the way, this engine lost its cab. Both photographs, Harry Gunderson Collection.

was to the north of Silver City, the line began at the smelter on the south side of town, swung around Boston Hill, passing through Chloride Flat (an old mining district), then continued north near the old sanatorium and over the pass in the Pinos Altos Mountains to the south side of the town. In all the distance measured about 12 miles.

Just after Christmas 1905, some 50 Silver City people enjoyed a Sunday afternoon excursion to the end of track, by then approaching Lankford's ranch. The return trip required 40 minutes, in deference to safety, but the trip was recorded as a "cold but happy" experience. In the middle of April 1906, the narrow gauge was reported to be practically completed with the rails now only $1^1/_2$ miles from the Pacific mine, the property of the Comanche company and the largest producer. Two additional Shays had been shipped from Lima, Ohio, and a number of ore cars had been acquired.

Financially, the Comanche Mining and Smelting Company was having difficulties. The sharp break in metal prices in the depression beginning in the fall of 1907 forced the company into bankruptcy and terminated operations of the railroad. Another victim of these reverses was the proposed 20-mile branch from Silver City to Tyrone where the parent company held copper property.

A new company, the Savanna Copper Company, took over the assets in October 1909, but no further work was done to extend the railroad. Some improvements were said to be made to the roadbed in 1910 but the revived operations were short-lived, followed by dismantling of the railroad.

Tyrone

One of the older copper mining districts in the Southwest is located in the Burro Mountains, about ten miles southwest of Silver City. Organized mining and smelting of copper in this area began in 1881 and a succession of companies worked the various claims with little sustained success. With money from two Chicago brothers named Leopold, a mining man named Carter organized the Burro Mountain Copper Company in 1904 and began working the St. Louis and other claims. Their mining

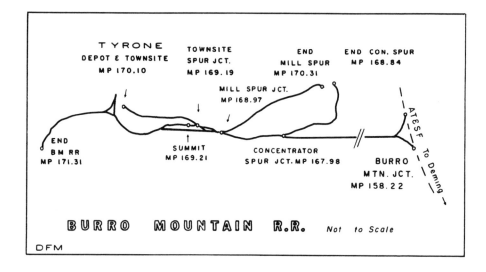

TYRONE
DEPOT & TOWNSITE
MP 170.10

TOWNSITE
SPUR JCT.
MP 169.19

END
MILL SPUR
MP 170.31

END CON. SPUR
MP 168.84

MILL SPUR JCT.
MP 168.97

END
BM RR
MP 171.31

SUMMIT
MP 169.21

CONCENTRATOR
SPUR JCT. MP 167.98

BURRO
MTN. JCT.
MP 158.22

ATESF

To Deming

BURRO   MOUNTAIN   R.R.   Not to Scale

DFM

camp took the name of Leopold and a 250-ton concentrator was built.

Soon after this event, Phelps Dodge acquired an interest in the company and full ownership in 1909. Some distances away from Leopold, the Chemung Copper Company was developing its mines near (old) Tyrone. Eventually this property, as well as other claims, was purchased by Phelps Dodge as that company planned extensive development of the copper district.

In 1913, plans were made for a new townsite to be called Tyrone and at the same time work began on the Burro Mountain Railroad. Thirteen miles in length, it was built in the interests of the EP&SW from Burro Mountain Junction, a point on the Silver City branch of the Santa Fe, to Tyrone. Though not finished until February 8, 1914, it had been leased to its parent, EP&SW, since the first of that year. As part of the plan to link Tyrone with the rest of the EP&SW, a connection was built from Deming to Whitney Junction (1.6 miles) and trackage rights were obtained over the Santa Fe branch for the intervening 33 miles to Burro Mountain Junction.

At the west end of the BMRR, there was a "townsite spur" almost a mile in length to serve the widely acclaimed model mining town of Tyrone built during 1917–18. The main line, parallel and south of the townsite, continued on a westerly course through the low hills to terminate in Niagara Gulch.

Phelps Dodge engaged Bertram G. Goodhue, an architect famed for his large cathedrals, to design buildings for the new townsite of Tyrone. During 1917, various buildings were erected. Among them were the general office, the P-D Mercantile store, EP&SW freight and passenger depots, and post office. The bank and building for independent stores were erected the following year. **Phelps Dodge Corporation, c. 1921.**

Two miles east of Niagara Gulch, another spur took off from the main line to the concentration mill which commenced work in 1916. (The Silver City map indictes the lines as of 1916.)

Though the mining town was widely praised, its useful life was unexpectedly short for the severe erosion of copper prices following World War I forced the closing of the property April 1, 1921. The railroad struggled on, hoping that the mines would be reopened, with the operation of a train each Wednesday from Hermanas to Deming to Tyrone and return. Even that had

With the general consolidation into the Phelps Dodge Corporation in May 1917, the Burro Mountain Copper Company already a subsidiary, became a division of P-D. Built by Westinghouse, the electric locomotive, BMCCo. No. 1, is shown with ore cars at the Niagara Tunnel. Phelps Dodge Corporation.

to come to an end. In 1934, with no expectation that Tyrone would ever again be an active mining town, the branch was abandoned and trackage rights relinquished.

Some decades later, with new mining and metallurgy in mind, the management of Phelps Dodge undertook a churn-drilling campaign to see if the property could be successfully operated by modern methods. After extensive drilling and analysis, which began in 1952, Phelps Dodge decided to reopen the property but this time, instead of an underground mine, it was to be a large open pit operation. Part of the development of the property called for a railroad, so Phelps Dodge set out

During 1919, copper production was curtailed and, on April 1, 1921, ceased entirely, not to be resumed for 40 years. The cessation of work caused a general exodus, and Tyrone became a ghost town. This is the last train leaving town. John G. Harlan Collection.

to rebuild the old railroad. Except at the west end of the line where a rearrangement of the mine and facilities brought a change in the location of the railroad, the old BMRR grade was used. The first train came to Tyrone over the renewed 12-mile branch on March 1, 1967. As an industrial spur, the Santa Fe moves cars in and out to connect with their trains destined to or from Deming and Rincon.

A subsequent development was the construction of the Hidalgo smelter in southwestern New Mexico by Phelps Dodge together with its own 35-mile standard-gauge railroad. The railroad, extending southerly from an unnamed switch just east of Separ on the Southern Pacific main line, was opened in February 1975.

The Santa Fe branch to Lake Valley approached under the late morning shadow of Monument Peak but, according to an 1885 map, the line was "under construction" for another 25 miles to Hillsboro and Kingston, a dream never to be realized. At the end of the branch was a wye track and, by a westward extension of

its tail track, trains followed the contour north and above the town,
passed the station, and ended with a half switchback at the mill.
Two spur tracks curve around the hill (left) *to the depot and mill,*
which are behind the photographer. Museum of New Mexico.

Having arrived, AT&SF No. 47 spots the passenger coach at the station and switches the three freight cars. Soon the mixed train will be readied for the return trip to the junction at Nutt and the terminal at Rincon. The locomotive reflects the Santa Fe renumbering of 1900. **Museum of New Mexico.**

Lake Valley

Among the more active silver mining towns of the last century which brought fame to New Mexico, Lake Valley, Hillsboro and Kingston were well known. When the Santa Fe built to Deming in 1881, the station of Nutt, named for H. C. Nutt, President of the A&P Railroad, was soon established to serve as the transfer point. Here supplies for the mining towns were taken from the cars and reloaded in the ponderous freight wagons for the last part of the trip.

Lake Valley grew up following the silver discovery in 1878, but one of the high points in the town's history was uncovering of one of the richest single bodies of silver ore ever found which was given the romantic name of the Bridal Chamber. The spirit of that particular day was dampened when it was learned that the general manager of the mines, George Daly, was killed by Apaches a scant six miles from town.

Under the name of The New Mexican Railroad Company, the Santa Fe constructed a 13-mile branch from Nutt to Lake Valley where it was welcomed on April 5, 1884.

The production of silver at Lake Valley was great but it was brief. After 1894, there was little activity in Lake Valley and almost no production after 1905. The mining districts beyond and the livestock business supported the branch but, as times changed, traffic dwindled and the branch was abandoned in 1934.

Zuni Mountain Railroad's "Four Spot" near Rock Dam Camp (later Breece) as it came out of Cottonwood Canyon. George Zimmerman photograph.

LUMBER RAILROADS

Narrow-Gauge Lumber Railroads of Rio Arriba County

In 1919, there were 175 miles of logging railroads in New Mexico and the lumber industry employed 1,300 people. A strong representation of these totals was accounted for by narrow-gauge railroads branching off the D&RG to tap timber in Rio Arriba County. Principal lines ran south from Chama and Dulce and north and south from Lumberton, N.M.

The first lumber spurs in New Mexico were built by the D&RG in 1888. One ran south from Chama (also called Biggs Jct.) for three miles to bring logs to the E. M. Biggs sawmill located at the southern edge of that town. Operated by the lumber people (some say under the name of Tierra Amarilla and Southern Railway) it was extended almost 12 miles to Tierra Amarilla in 1896. An additional ten miles of track southeast and east along Nutrias Creek were necessary to reach new stands of timber.

By 1902, the timber around Tierra Amarilla had been cut over so the track material was moved to Lumberton where, in a cooperative effort, the D&RG and the Burns-Biggs Lumber

Company built a 33-mile railroad to El Vado. In August 1903, ten miles of track had been laid to Horse Lake and grading had been completed for another five miles. It was expected that the tracks would reach El Vado on October 1 so that the mill could be set up at its new location.

Although a seven-mile extension to Gallina had been projected for early construction, this did not take place until 1918. Again the entire branch was operated by the lumber company (except for approximately five years ending in 1914 when it was dormant), this time under the name of the Rio Grande Southwestern Railroad.

The lumber company usually built about six miles of logging spurs each year. One continued south almost 20 miles to Llaves while others went in the opposite direction along Willow Creek. In 1928, after the available timber along the 40-mile line to El Vado and Gallina had been exhausted, this railroad was dismantled. The lumber company, now the New Mexico Lumber Company, a subsidiary of McPhee and McGinnity, moved its operations the same year to McPhee, four miles from Dolores, Colorado.

While Biggs was cutting around Tierra Amarilla, he was also logging north of Lumberton, New Mexico. For transportation purporses, he incorporated the Rio Grande and Pagosa Springs Railroad in 1895 to build from Lumberton to Pagosa Springs, Colorado, a distance of about 38 miles. In the same year, Biggs graded and laid track from Lumberton to Edith, just over the line in Colorado, where a lumber camp was established. From here a branch went east to Chromo while the main line continued north, a few miles being built every few years. Blanco was reached in 1903 and the next year an eight-mile extension placed the terminus at Flaugh, only a few miles east of Pagosa Springs and 30 miles from Lumberton.

Connecting with this railroad were logging spurs and the whole operation was really part of the New Mexico Lumber Company. The road never quite reached Pagosa Springs and, beginning in 1911, the operated mileage began shrinking. By the end of 1914, the company was practically out of business; the mill was shut down, most of the tracks had been pulled and the equipment was being used on the Rio Grande Southwestern.

Pagosa Springs did have its railroad but it came from a different direction with a different corporate name. Built by the Pagosa Lumber Company under the name of The Rio Grande, Pagosa and Northern Railroad Company in 1900 from Pagosa Junction (Gato), Colorado, to Pagosa (31 miles), the property was conveyed to the D&RG in 1908 in accordance with a previous agreement and was abandoned in 1936.

The same Pagosa Lumber Company, a subsidiary of the Newton Lumber Company (of Colorado) until 1918, also operated southwest of Dulce, New Mexico, for a number of years. To bring the logs to its sawmill at Dulce, it built some trackage southwest of the town, some prior to World War I and more in 1923, eventually reaching Mills Lake. Operations were terminated around 1930.

Zuni Mountain Railroad— The McGaffey Company

The building of the Atlantic and Pacific Railroad opened up several stands of timber in Arizona and New Mexico, one important location being the Zuni Mountains, forming part of the Continental Divide. Located south and west of Grants and Thoreau, this area is now part of the Cibola National Forest.

In 1890, the Mitchell Brothers of Michigan bought some 300,000 acres of timber land from the A&P Railroad. Honoring these men, the railroad established the station of Mitchell where the lumber company built a sawmill the following year. To tap the timber, the Mitchell Brothers built a narrow-gauge railroad for about six miles southwest to their camp of Square Wells and from there various logging spurs were built into the mountains.

The Mitchell Brothers closed down after a few years and, around the turn of the century, the property passed into the hands of Ohio and Michigan men who formed the American Lumber Company in 1901. A number of changes then took place. The station of Mitchell became Thoreau, the sawmill was moved over 125 miles to a new site on the north side of Albuquerque and the railroad, now the Zuni Mountain Railroad, was changed to standard gauge and extended.

When the American Lumber Company was formed in 1901, it widened the tracks of the Zuni Mountain Railroad to standard-gauge and established a new camp ten miles above Kettner called Sawyer in honor of W. H. Sawyer of Hillsdale, Michigan, the president of the lumber company.

First logging operations of the American Lumber Company were west of Cottonwood Cañon and the wider gauge railroad enabled a train of Zuni Mountain Railroad cars to be switched off the logging line to the Santa Fe to be hauled to Albuquerque. The first train of 30 cars, piled high with white pine logs, dumped their load into the log pound and the new Albuquerque sawmill began cutting October 23, 1903.

As the timber areas were cut over, the railroad was extended along the east side of Oso Ridge (the Continental Divide) halting at Kettner where a base camp was established. A few years later the camp was moved to Sawyer, a site named in honor of the president of the firm. About 1911 tracks were pushed on to Paxton Springs and Agua Fria, about 36 miles from Thoreau

Outfit cars for the loggers at Rock Dam Camp, which was largely populated by Navajos. Paddy Martinez became a well-known Navajo after his discoveries of uranium near Grants, New Mexico. Paddy, the tall man with the large hat in the left side of the picture, is standing behind two seated men. **George Zimmerman photograph.**

bringing the total length of the railroad, including branches and spurs, to 55 miles.

The American Lumber Company shut down in 1913 and went into receivership the following year. All was quiet until a new company, the McKinley Land and Lumber Company, took over about 1917. This company was a subsidiary of The West Virginia Timber Company which was headed by George E. Breece. Additional timber lands were acquired and lumbering was resumed. A new camp, first called Rock Dam Camp and later Breece, was established about a half dozen miles from Thoreau. Reflecting the new order, operations were carried out under the G. E. Breece Lumber Company beginning about 1924. Spur tracks to various cutting areas were of temporary duration being moved about as required with most of the work being done by Zuni Indians. Logging operations were conducted by Navajo Indians and Mexicans.

The "Four Spot" came to grief when it was pushed off the coal chute at Rock Dam Camp. George Zimmerman photograph.

George E. Breece was an important lumberman in this area. Locomotive No. 9 once had an active life on the Colorado Midland, but it had been relegated to storage in the back of an engine house at Grants when it was photographed in 1939. Ted Wurm photograph.

This 2-6-2T, No. 7, was one of a pair built by H. K. Porter for the McKinley Land & Lumber Company. In place of the usual tender, the fuel oil tank was behind the cab and two large water tanks were mounted on each side of the boiler. It had become G. E. Breece Lumber Company No. 7 when photographed at Grants in 1939. **Ted Wurm photograph.**

Much of the output of timber found its way into railroad cross ties which were cut to the appropriate size in the mountains by Buck Moore and George Zimmerman, independent contractors, and sold to the AT&SF which took them to their tie treating plant at Albuquerque, 125 miles from Thoreau. Shortening the length of haul was a factor in relocating the Zuni Mountain Railroad and in 1926 a new line was built from Grants, 30 miles east of Thoreau, through Zuni Cañon to Paxton Springs, about 20 miles from Grants. The old line from Thoreau was dismantled. Breece continued operations until the fall of 1931 when poor market conditions closed down lumbering. (Breece had also been operating at Alamogordo.)

Two years later, M. R. Prestridge and Carl Seligman, formerly associated with Breece, reopened the logging area and moved west into a new timber zone. From a point near Paxton Springs, another 17 miles of railroad were built over the Continental Divide, along the southwestern side of the ridge to a point five miles beyond Tinaja (near El Morro) and about 42 miles from Grants. Prestridge and Seligman discontinued work

Built by Lima in 1912, this three-truck Shay served The McGaffey Company for many years around Perea, near Gallup, before being sent to Durango, Mexico. **Robert E. Searle Collection.**

in 1940, the scrap dealers moved in and by 1942 the last of the lumber railroads in the Zuni Mountains was nothing but a memory.

Midway between Gallup and Thoreau on the Santa Fe is the station of Perea where connection was made with the railroad of The McGaffey Company. South of Perea were the properties of the company including the town of McGaffey and a sawmill, both a dozen miles by rail from Perea. Beyond the lumber town the logging railroad crept southward, building a few miles at a time to reach new stands of timber. Working along the west side of the ridge, the railroad was built to Page and finally to Dam Valley, a distance of 17 miles from McGaffey. A. B. McGaffey sold out around 1930 but, after fifteen years of lumbering, the land had been pretty well cut over. It was about the time of the slump in house building and the property soon

Though logging railroads in New Mexico had long since been relegated to history, the New Mexico Timber Company retained a gasoline-powered switch for use in its Bernalillo lumber yard in October 1959. Note the standard coupler and air brake hose. **Fred M. Springer photograph.**

became a candidate for abandonment. Had the line been extended another ten or fifteen miles, it would have been possible to connect with the Prestridge and Seligman railroad near Tinaja and a second railroad, 85 miles long from Perea to Grants, would have been formed.

Cloudcroft in the Sacramento Mountains

Lumbering in the Sacramento Mountains on anything but a small scale was not possible until Charles Eddy built his El Paso and Northeastern and the branch line, Alamogordo and Sacramento Railway, in 1898–99. There had been other mills such as La Luz Saw Mill at Tularosa in 1881 and the Peñasco

The Alamogordo Lumber Company operated the pioneer logging railroad in the Sacramento Mountains. Stiff grades necessitated a geared locomotive, and Lima built this Shay in 1902. Ownership of the lumber company and the railroad passed to the Sacramento Mountain Lumber Company, which was followed by the Southwest Lumber Company in 1921. In all cases the locomotive remained the No 5. Bert H. Ward Collection.

Lumber Company in the 1890s but the absence of transportation limited sales to local markets.

With the building of the A&SM, the picture changed as the railroad provided access to outside markets. Though a number of companies have operated logging railroads around Cloudcroft since 1898, they can be divided into two groups, each composed of several companies with one succeeding the other. Like the A&SM, all the tracks were of standard gauge.

The earliest group had its beginnings as the Alamogordo Lumber Company which was formed in May 1898 by men identified with the Lackawanna Lumber Company of Pennsylvania as well as the Mississippi Central Railroad and lumbering in Mississippi. During the summer of 1898, while the A&SM was under construction, the lumber company built a boarding house for 50 employees and began work on its lumber manu-

Steam shovel No. 1 of the Cloudcroft Lumber and Land Company was dumping a load into a horse-drawn wagon, presumably for filling a swale, when this photograph was taken. **Dorothy Neal Collection.**

facturing plant at Alamogordo, said to be the largest built in the Rocky Mountain region up to that time.

First logging tracks of the Alamogordo Lumber Company were built from Cox Canyon where the A&SM reached that point in 1899. Four years later, when the A&SM stretched to Russia, a few miles away, the lumber company built tracks into the woods from that terminal. In all logging mileage totaled about 15 miles in 1915 and tracks were located and relocated into new timber cutting areas as needed. Logging cars moved over the logging spurs to Russia where the cars were switched into A&SM trains destined to the sawmill at Alamogordo. From here the finished lumber was shipped to market.

The fortunes of the Alamogordo Lumber Company waned about 1914 and in 1918 the sawmill and other property was

The camp of the Southwest Lumber Company in Pumphouse Canyon, about two miles east of Cloudcroft. The slide (left) brings logs down Rawlins Canyon. Dorothy Neal Collection.

taken over by the Sacramento Mountain Lumber Company. Adversities continued, the new company suffered the loss of the big mill at Alamogordo by fire only a few months after the change in ownership.

Two years later, the new company was acquired by the Southwest Lumber Company which also purchased the remaining property of the Alamogordo Lumber Company. Southwest rebuilt the mill at Alamogordo where production began in May 1921. Camp Marcia, about six miles south of Russia, was logging headquarters with repair shops and offices. The locomotive roster listed Shay and Heisler locomotives which had been passed on from one corporate ownership to the next.

The Southwest Lumber Company, under the management of Louis Carr of North Carolina, utilized the logging railroad in its operations until 1942 (part of it was not dismantled until 1945) with tracks running in and out of the canyons south of Marcia all the way down to Agua Chiquita. East of Marcia, the Southwest railroad went down to Peñasco Canyon for about ten miles with important spurs reaching into Dark Canyon and Willis Canyon. Reports as to the length of tracks operated in 1927 vary from 16 to 24 miles but, in any event, Southwest Lumber, employing 300 men was a major factor in Otero County. Much of the production from their mill on Eighth Street in Alamogordo was in the form of railroad ties. Conveniently adjoining the mill was the railroad tie treating plant, dating back to the early days and continuing in service until about 1958.

The second succession of lumber companies began in 1920 when Ben Longwell and C. M. Pate formed the Cloudcroft Lumber and Land Company to cut timber in the Mescalero Apache Indian Reservation under a contract.

From Cloudcroft, the new company built a logging railroad in a northerly direction over the range then into the timber areas along Silver Spring Canyon in 1924 and eventually to Elk Canyon. Unavoidable delays in the commencement of lumber operations placed such a heavy strain on the company's finances that it was forced into receivership in 1926. The property was sold to the George E. Breece Lumber Company which operated in the Zuni Mountains in western New Mexico as well as in Louisiana. The Breece management built a new mill, planing mill and box factory on 14th Street in Alamogordo in

1926–27 and extended the railroad into Elk Canyon and some of its tributaries.

Even before the depression of the 1930s, the lumber business of the Southwest did not enjoy as much prosperity as had been anticipated. The new Breece mill operated only a few years before it was shut down, most of it taking on a ghostly appearance as only a portion was active during the 1930s. Dismantling of the railroad took place in 1940 and the remaining property was acquired the next year by the M. R. Prestridge Company. The latter company, which purchased the Southwest Lumber Company in 1945, found trucks more suitable for its operations which were continued in the Sacramento Mountains for another fifteen years.

Tales of horrendous operations over multi-laced switchbacks, runaway cars, boiler explosions and adventures in the woods—some comic, others tragic—are all part of the great days of logging in the Sacramento Mountains. Though lumbering still continues in these mountains, the shrill whistle and the sharp bark of the engine exhaust have not been heard for almost a generation, but they will remain as part of the heritage of New Mexico.

Cimarron and Northwestern Railway Company

Though the lumber operators working along the Canadian River on the northern edge of New Mexico did not prosper as they had expected when the Colorado and Southern put in their Catskill branch, there were other areas which, in the eyes of Thomas A. Schomberg, held promise.

Reaching southwest from Raton, New Mexico, the St. Louis, Rocky Mountain and Pacific Railway had completed its line to Cimarron. In 1907, this road was pushing its line to Ute Park and, hopefully, beyond. It was at this time that Schomberg formed The Continental Tie and Lumber Company to conduct operations in the Ponil Park area of the Maxwell Grant and the Cimarron and Northwestern Railway Company was formed as a subsidiary of the lumber company. Originally, it was projected to Van Bremmer Park with a branch to the timber areas, a plan

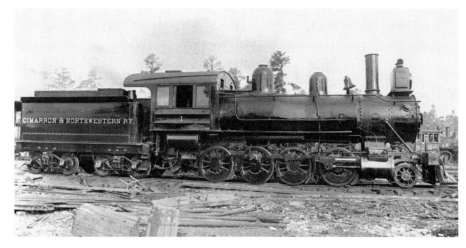

Freshly repainted, this former Pennsylvania 2-8-0 was on the roster of the Cimarron & Northwestern Railway for many years as it operated between Cimarron and Bonito. G. M. Best photograph, D. S. Richer Collection.

involving some 50 miles of railroad but actual construction was carried out on a more modest basis.

Work began at the town of Cimarron early in the spring of 1907 and the grading and track forces worked up the canyon of North Ponil Creek for 22 miles to Ponil Park where the first train pulled up in January 1908. Ponil Park was the terminus for three years until the tracks were pushed ahead for 13 miles to form a large loop ending at Bonito. Ownership of the extension was vested in the name of The Continental Tie and Lumber Company but the C&NW operated its trains over this new section, thus being able to boast of a 35-mile railroad.

Stands of timber were cut over and the logs found their way into mine timbers around Raton, cross ties for the railroad in the area and into buildings of various kinds. As sections of timber lands were exhausted, adjoining segments of the railroad no longer witnessed logging cars being shunted to loading platforms and eventually parts of the railroad were abandoned. First to go were eight miles of the Bonito extension in 1916. Other abandonments followed. In 1923, when the C&NW sought and obtained ICC approval to abandon 14 miles of line from Ponil Park to South Ponil (located at the confluence of North and South Ponil Creeks), nobody cared to enter a protest. This left the C&NW with only 7.5 miles of road, extending from South Ponil to Cimarron, where the lumber company operated a tie treating plant.

Even before ICC approval had been obtained for the abandonment, construction was underway on a ten-mile spur of the Continental Tie and Lumber along South Ponil Creek to the Wilson Mesa area. As in the case of the other lines serving timber areas, the expected life of this spur was limited but there was another threat to bring the entire railroad's existence rapidly to a close, for the CT&L management found that logging trucks were more suitable for their operations. So back to the ICC went the attorneys of the C&NW seeking authority to abandon the entire line. Lumber had become of even greater importance to the railroad; in 1929 over 97% of the 6,307 tons of freight handled were classified as forest products, so that the remaining commodities represented an insignificant amount of traffic. The ICC granted the request and the entire line was abandoned on October 31, 1930 while the CT&L continued operations in the area for another seven years.

Santa Barbara Tie and Pole Company

Lumber and logs are transported in various ways by different lumber companies; the Santa Barbara Tie and Pole Company probably employed nearly all of the possible combinations except the aerial tramway. From the stands of timber to the sawmill in the mountains and to the tie treating plant in Albuquerque, a number of methods were used: horses, log chutes, V-flumes, a narrow-gauge railroad, the booming down the Rio Grande and finally a specially built standard-gauge branch to connect with the main line at Domingo, New Mexico.

Formed in 1907 by a Vermonter named A. B. McGaffey to supply cross ties to the Santa Fe under contract, the Santa Barbara Tie and Pole Company cut timber on the Santa Barbara Grant, about 40 miles north of the territorial capital. (After operating the plant for a few years, McGaffey sold the SBT&P to the Santa Fe and subsequently had his own operation in the Zuni Mountains.)

The Santa Barbara Tie and Pole Company operated this narrow-gauge Shay in Northern New Mexico. Later, it was shipped to Nevada for use on the Pioche-Pacific Railroad. D. S. Richter Collection.

Logs were brought to the sawmill at Hodges on the Rio Santa Barbara (to be cut into ties) by one of several forms of transport. A narrow-gauge railroad, built in the early days of the operation, brought logs to the sawmill from two directions. One line ran up Rio Chiquito Canyon while the other ran north of Rio Santa Barbara to Llano Llegua. From the sawmill, cut ties were floated down the rivers to the meeting with the Rio Grande where they were held until the most propitious time. The ties were then boomed down the Rio Grande through White Rock Canyon to Cochiti where they were lifted from the river by a large boom to waiting gondolas at the terminus of a Santa Fe branch locally called the Domingo and Rio Grande Railroad.

Boom, the name given the north end of the eleven-mile branch, consisted of nothing more than three company houses, loading facilities and a wye track. Boom was a bustle of activity for a 30-day period each year when the ties were sent down the river. The time was usually around the last week of June and continued into July. At Boom, coal cars loaded with the ties were switched into trains for the journey to the main line at Domingo. Because of the 4% grades on this branch, it was usually necessary to "double" the hills. At Domingo, the cars were moved in main line trains to Albuquerque where the ties were treated in the creosoting plant and from there distributed along the railroad. Domingo had been known as Thornton prior to November 1905. Thornton itself was the result of a name change; previously the station had been called Wallace. In 1884 timetables, a meal stop was indicated at Wallace and a map in *Poor's Manual* of 1891 showed Wallace at the end of a projected Rio Grande Southern line from Durango.

The year of the demise of the standard-gauge line is 1928 when only 106,000 ties were boomed down the Rio Grande in lieu of the usual 400,000 ties.

As to the narrow-gauge railroad part of this operation, its termination date is uncertain at this writing. It appears to have been around 1916. The solitary Shay locomotive traveled to other places, including Pioche, Nevada, where it had been photographed many times. It was last reported on display at a museum at one of the hotels in Las Vegas, Nevada.

Hallack & Howard Lumber Company

Two sets of brothers, the Hallacks of Denver and the Howards from Chicago, joined forces in Denver in 1877 as the Hallack & Howard Lumber Company. Operating a retail business at first, the company subsequently went into logging at Mancos, Colorado, on the Rio Grande Southern, and at Arloa during the first few years of this century. The second decade found the firm in New Mexico where they had bought 117 million board feet in the Carson National Forest. Headquarters were established at La Madera (Spanish for wood) which was at the end of a new D&RG branch connecting with its line to Santa Fe.

From La Madera, even before the D&RG had completed its branch in 1914, work had begun on the logging railroad which extended 15 miles up Potrero Canyon. Grading was done with approximately 100 two-horse teams but half-sized scrapers had to be used as this was all the little Indian ponies could handle. When regular lumbering was in full sway, horses were used to bring logs to the railroad or short spurs branching out from the line (often a half to a full mile long) over which steam trains

Halleck & Howard No. 5 operated on its own narrow-gauge log-ging railroad and connected with the La Madera branch of the Denver & Rio Grande Western. W. J. Duteau photograph, J. P. Here-ford, Jr., Collection, c. 1921.

brought the loaded cars to the sawmill at La Madera.

About 1922 another line was built by H&H, this one to Vallecitos, using steel reclaimed from the first line of railroad. In addition to the sawmill, H&H also operated a planing mill and box factory at La Madera. Boxes were shipped "knocked down" to the San Luis Valley for vegetables and to Lamar, also in Colorado, for packing Rocky Ford cantaloupes.

Motive power consisted of rod locomotives bought or leased from the D&RG and C&S and geared locomotives—a Heisler and a new Climax.

What had been expected to be a timber stand capable of supporting a 25-year cutting operation proved to be disappointing as it was exhausted in about half that time. La Madera closed down in 1927 and H&H operations were moved to Cascade, Idaho. Operations there were sold to Boise Cascade in 1960.

Santa Fe Northwestern Railway and Cuba Extension Railroad

Probably the last and certainly the longest independent railroad built in New Mexico after World War I was the Santa Fe Northwestern Railway. It was the lumber railroad of The White Pine Lumber Company, headed by Guy A. Porter and managed by his son, Frank H. Porter. Associated for a time with the Porters was George E. Breece who later logged west of Grants.

This railroad was built during 1922–24 from Bernalillo, a station on the AT&SF near Albuquerque, northwest to San Ysidro, thence north to Jemez and Deer Creek (41 miles) to tap the timber in the Cañon de San Diego Grant. Beyond that point, The White Pine Lumber Company railroad continued up the canyon for another six miles to the main camp of Porter. From Porter, saddle-tank locomotives ran up various canyons as the track builders followed the logging operations. In 1926, the interchange between the logging road and the SFNW was moved to Porter, then a camp of 300 people, because of the better topography, at which time the SFNW acquired trackage rights over the additional six miles.

For a short line, the SFNW was expensive to build—over

The Santa Fe Northwestern was a lumber railroad extending north from Bernalillo with a roster of miscellaneous locomotives. No. 107 was photographed by Ted Wurm at Bernalillo in the summer of 1939.

After going into bankruptcy and forcing its S&NW Railway to fold, the White Pine Lumber Company reorganized as the New Mexico Lumber & Timber Company. The latter's Heisler, No. 105, posed here at Bernalillo in July 1939. Built in 1929, the Heisler ended up with the Southwest Lumber Mills at McNary, Arizona. Bert H. Ward Collection.

$1,000,000 was spent in construction. Leaving Bernalillo, the location of the sawmill of The White Pine Lumber Company, the railroad crossed the Rio Grande on a trestle and then traversed a sandy stretch, where drifting sand often hampered operations in spite of sand fences. At times it was necessary to send out a section crew ahead of the train to clear the sand off the tracks. Farther up the canyon there were two short tunnels, partly lined with timber.

For a time the operation prospered. To supply the mill from which sash and other finished lumber items were sent to the Midwest, a number of locomotives were necessary. In 1928, about 20 miles of logging spurs were operated with motive power consisting of one Heisler and one Climax. Two rod locomotives were used on the SFNW. The locomotive roster was lengthened in 1930 with the addition of another Heisler and two rod locmotives.

Shortly after the new power had been acquired, the decline in residential construction began, finally forcing the lumber company into bankruptcy. Emerging as the New Mexico Lumber & Timber Company, a change of operation followed by which trucks were substituted for logging spurs. The SFNW, as part of this change, shrunk to 38 miles when the log-loading platform was established at Gilman in 1937. Even this abbreviated railroad had only a short life remaining; in May 1941 operations ceased as the Guadalupe and Jemez Rivers went on a rampage, washing out three miles of track and damaging several bridges. The cost of rehabilitating the railroad was more than could be justified and ICC approval for abandonment of the line was granted. A little over a mile of track was left in place for switching purposes at the sawmill (the company was now the New Mexico Timber Company) and the lumber company switched cars with a diesel.

Another railroad, this one built to serve a coal mine, branched off the SFNW at San Ysidro to go west and north to La Ventana and to a point five miles beyond, in all, 33 miles being built. Organized as the Cuba Extension Railroad in 1923, its proposed line was to extend to Cuba, a small trading center with an adjoining prospective copper mine, 44 miles from San Ysidro. (There was also the unrealized hope of continuing on to Farmington or Durango.)

The corporate life of the Cuba Extension Railroad was short. Though its name was changed to the Santa Fe Northern Railroad, this measure failed to prevent the road from being sold at foreclosure in 1928 to be reorganized as the Santa Fe, San Juan & Northern Railroad.

Built in the interests of the San Juan Coal & Coke Company, operating mines at La Ventana, the coal company during 1928–29 operated the road as a private carrier, delivering about 15 cars of coal a week to the SFNW at San Ysidro.

Arrangements were made in 1929 for expansion and ICC approval was obtained as a prerequisite. Trackage rights over the SFNW between San Ysidro and Bernalillo augmented the operation by 24 miles. Though the ICC authorized the company to build to Cuba no additional construction was undertaken.

In 1930, the SFSJ&N operated as a common carrier for nine months, handled 857 cars and reported a respectable $70,143 in revenues. Then the storms came with crippling washouts and, to make matters worse, there was no money for repairs readily available. Most months of 1931 and 1932, the road was idle. Repairs, made after a storm, would keep the road alive until the next deluge, then the process of finding the money rehabilitating the road would start all over again. Following the pattern of many larger railroads, this short line applied to the Reconstruction Finance Corporation (RFC) for a loan of $50,000 for repairs. The amount was small but the likelihood of repayment was even smaller so the request was denied. Old timers cannot recall any operation of the line after the big storm; certainly the removal of all the rails in 1940–41 terminated any possible hope of resumption of service over the Santa Fe, San Juan & Northern.

The hotel at Montezuma (Las Vegas Hot Springs) was served by the Las Vegas & Hot Springs Electric Railway, Light & Power Company. In this carefully posed picture of 1904, all of its equipment is congregated on Bridge Street in Las Vegas. Museum of New Mexico Collection.

STREETCARS IN NEW MEXICO

Las Vegas

Smaller cities of the Western United States in the pre-automobile days generally had little need for public transit. Closely contained geographically, the usual small town could be crossed on foot from one end to the other with little difficulty. It was only when there was some special attraction some little distance away that a horse car line would be established. In New Mexico, only two cities had streetcar lines though others were candidates at various times.

Las Vegas has been two separate towns for many years—a situation which was changed by the March 1970 election approving consolidation. The old town, west of the Gallinas Creek, dates back to the days of Mexican rule while the new town (at one time called East Las Vegas) came into existence with the arrival of the Santa Fe Railway.

That the two communities should be linked by organized transit was the objective of the Las Vegas & Hot Springs Railway Company in 1880. Services on the line, according to an unflattering report in 1886, were described as "very indifferent"

Albuquerque, in its early years, boasted of a horse-car line shown here at the corner of First and Central on a quiet day. University of New Mexico Collection.

as one could walk from one town to the other in less time required than by waiting for the tardy cars.

Las Vegas was also the point of beginning of the nine-mile branch built by the Santa Fe in 1882 along Gallinas Creek to the hot springs and continuing another two miles to the ice ponds. The curative waters of the Montezuma Hot Springs, as they were called, and the large hotel drew a distinguished clientele from all over the world. Burned twice, the hotel was rebuilt each time but eventually it lost favor and was closed in 1903. It was then used for various purposes, including a seminary and, since 1981, a campus of the United World College.

In 1902, the Las Vegas and Hot Springs Electric Railway, Light and Power Company was incorporated and the electric line was opened the next year. For the benefit of the uninformed the letterhead of the company, after giving the corporate title, including the following statement:

"Ten miles of an electric railway is now in operation between Casteñeda Hotel, East Las Vegas, and the 'Montezuma' Las Vegas hot springs. The finest climate and the most beautiful scenic route in the world."

A portion of the line was operated over the Santa Fe branch under a lease arrangement, the electric railway stringing overhead wires for the trolleys.

East Las Vegas, where the Santa Fe maintained a roundhouse (now closed) and an early tie-treating plant, was also a division point. While these activities contributed passengers for the electric line, it was special events, such as the Brotherhood of Locomotive Firemen's Ball on July 3, 1903 at the hot springs, that boosted the traffic. People came from points as far away as Albuquerque for the dance and special schedules were necessary to handle the crowd.

Financially, the company had its problems and several reorganizations were necessary. In 1905 it became the Las Vegas Railway and Power Company and four years later, it started its last lease on life as the Las Vegas Transit Company, a subsidiary of the Las Vegas Light and Power Company. A losing battle with autos forced the company to prepare for abandonment early in 1927. At the close of that year, Las Vegas Transit, by then reduced to three miles of track, ceased operations.

Several years before abandonment of the streetcar line, its

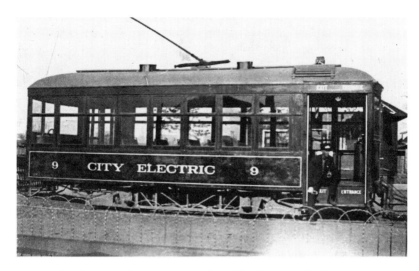

Animal-powered cars were replaced by the cars of Albuquerque Traction Company, but financial success eluded the company. It was reorganized as the City Electric Company. Car No. 9 was built by the St. Louis Car Company. **B. H. Ward Collection.**

lease of the Santa Fe branch had been terminated. (The streetcars had long ceased operating to Hot Springs.) Though its usefulness as a passenger line had long vanished, its operation as a freight branch of the Santa Fe was to continue for another ten years. the principal commodity was natural ice, formed in the ponds just beyond the hotel. For many years the Agua Pura Ice Company had shipped great quantities of ice to points as distant as El Paso, but mechanical refrigeration finally closed this business and the branch was abandoned in 1937.

Albuquerque

When the Santa Fe was coming to Albuquerque in 1880, they found the route by the Plaza originally contemplated necessitated a higher priced right of way than seemed justified, so the surveyors moved their stakes two miles to the east. A new town grew around the revised route and a horse car line was established to link the two communities.

Horse cars gave way to electric power about the start of this century. In 1905, the Albuquerque Traction Company (incorporated 1903) operated four cars over three miles of track from old Albuquerque to the new city and then south for a short distance to an area designated as Barelas. It was about this time that extensions were made. One went to the northern edge of the city to the sawmill of the American Lumber Company (cutting logs from the Zuni Mountains). When the other extension was built along Central Avenue (later US 66) as far as the university, the tracks totaled about six miles.

The traction business in Albuquerque was not a financial success and operations were conducted at a loss. In May 1915, the company was forced into receivership as it had outstanding bills of some $9,000 and only $1.09 in the bank. A new company called City Electric Company, a name not giving any clue of the locality, was formed and took over that fall.

An army camp during World War I brought a boom to the streetcar line as overflow crowds of soldiers rode the cars, hanging on to any possible hand-hold. After the war, this extra traffic evaporated and the competition of the auto began to take its toll, not only in lost patronage but also in demands from the city for a financial contribution for street paving. The matter was contested in litigation and the court found for the City of Albuquerque. In effect, it was a Pyrrhic victory for it hastened the demise of the streetcar lines. Finances were strained, the streetcar went into the hands of a receiver again in 1927 and all service was terminated at the end of that year, causing some concern for the motorettes who had been operating the cars since the war but were now without employment.

Though only two electric lines operated in New Mexico, proposals appeared in other communities. Among them was the two-mile line considered in 1903 from Alamogordo to the sanatorium. Three years later there was talk of linking Roswell and Carlsbad by a 75-mile electric railway. In the northwest corner of the territory, another 22-mile line would have extended west from Farmington to Jewitt, near Hogback Mountain. The capital city, Santa Fe, had various proposals for streetcars, including an electric line which blossomed and wilted around 1900–1901 only to be revived momentarily before being relegated to the forgotten past.

At the Southern Pacific (GH&SA) shops in El Paso, a locomotive boiler is being lowered on an engine frame.

EL PASO AND JUÁREZ

Not many streetcar lines are still operating west of Chicago today. But as late as 1973 one operated in El Paso. It crossed the Rio Grande to Juárez, one of Mexico's larger cities, and then returned to form a complete circle. As the cars operated in only one direction, it was undoubtedly the only car line in which a passenger, boarding in one part of a city and stepping off in another part of the same city (if already traversed by that streetcar) had to go through customs and immigration of two countries.

El Paso del Norte dates back to the days of the Spanish in the late 1500s and, located on the river, it has been the logical entry into New Mexico for centuries. When the area became part of the United States, that portion north of the Rio Grande went through a succession of names including Franklin, the name given the first post office which changed to El Paso in 1859.

Early railroad surveys found "the pass" a desirable location but it was not until the Southern Pacific arrived May 19, 1881 from the west that El Paso had its first train. At that time, the

Santa Fe was on its way down the Rio Grande from Albu-querque. The construction train locomotive was whistling on April 19 to announce its arrival in Doña Ana and in Las Cruces a few days later, people watched the driving of spikes as the rails came to their town.

Though the Santa Fe tracks did not reach El Paso until June 11, 1881, its president, T. Jefferson Coolidge, members of the Board of Directors and their wives left the comforts of their private car which they had boarded in Boston to continue their journey by stage to El Paso for a short visit back in March. Some of the directors had railroad interests in Mexico.

Under the name of The Galveston, Harrisburg and San An-tonio Railway, the Southern Pacific continued eastward, first meeting the T&P at Sierra Blanca later that year and its own forces, building from San Antonio, in January 1883. Within a few weeks after its arrival in El Paso in 1881, SP began work on terminal facilities. Initially, the 15-stall roundhouse, coal shed, passenger station and freight depot were erected with other buildings to follow.

El Paso was important to Southern Pacific as part of the route from the Pacific to the Atlantic as well as a trading center for southern New Mexico. To the Texas & Pacific, it was an important objective, achieved by joint use of the GH&SA (SP) line from Sierra Blanca, for the T&P gained another connection and, in the future would enjoy others. To the Santa Fe, El Paso was its key for the north and south route into Mexico. Across the river was the city of Paseo del Norte (changed to Juárez in September 1888 after a two-day program honoring the hero) and here men prominent in the managing of the destiny of the Santa Fe carried on an independent project under the name of the Mexican Central Railway.

Incorporated early in 1880, this railroad from Paso del Norte to Mexico City (1,224 miles) was built in four sections. Tracks of the northern segment were completed to Chihuahua (city) on September 14, 1882. The next day three Mexican Central trains left Paso del Norte with 600 passengers—many from New Mexico—for Chihuahua where the silver spike was driven the following day. The entire route to Mexico City was completed March 8, 1884.

With the Mexican Central in operation, people could go by

The El Paso & Southwestern, following the merger with the EP&NE, centralized its shops in El Paso, shown here (above) under construction in 1906. Prior to the merger, the SP (GH&SA) had separate shops.

No. 360. The Southern Pacific Company's Passenger Depot, El Paso, Texas.

R.R. EATING HOUSE & LUNCH COUNTER

Southern Pacific Trains El Paso Texas

These interesting views show early days in El Paso. The photograph shows the Southern Pacific depot, while the scene of the station grounds and yards below was taken by the same photographer, Turrill, from the second floor of the depot. Some passengers are watching their train being switched, while others are presumably fortifying themselves in the "R.R. Eatinghouse & Lunch Counter." Almost across the street was the popular Pierson Hotel. Three Turrill photographs, University of Texas at El Paso. Leon C. Metz Collection, c. 1880s. *The Santa Fe had its own depot at Sixth and South Santa Fe Streets* (opposite below).

No. 35e "The Pierson" El Paso, Texas

El Paso witnessed a variety of heavy steam power. Above, big 4-8-2 No. 906 is on T&P train No. 8. A fat-boilered old Santa Fe 2-10-2 dwarfs its small tender. All photographs, A. C. Phelps, 1947. The SP's (T&NO) 2-10-2 No. 989 (above) presents a more modern

appearance and looks a good bit faster. International operations add an unusual flavor to El Paso railroading. NdeM Pacific No. 2528 prepares to leave Juárez for Mexico City in 1947. All photographs A. C. Phelps.

The eastbound Golden State *passes through El Paso on February 20, 1948, powered by a diesel locomotive acquired for the SP's* Shasta Daylight, *which did not begin operations until its passenger cars were delivered the next year. Shortly after this picture was taken, work began on the three-year task of depressing the tracks in El Paso.*

rail in any one of four directions. By 1902, the choice was expanded as one could travel by one of two roads in each direction. To the east, passengers could take the SP (GH&SA) or the T&P, to the north there were the Santa Fe and the El Paso & Northeastern. The SP and the EP&SW competed for the Arizona business while to the south there were now two lines. The Rio Grande, Sierra Madre and Pacific Railroad, beginning construction in 1896, reached the Mormon settlement of Casas Grandes, 156 miles from Juarez, the following summer. Canadian interests took over the property in 1909, renaming it the Mexico North Western Railway, and in 1912, when the last rails

The architecture of the Union Station in El Paso has been modified in recent years. The peaked-roof of the tower has been removed, but the general lines of the building are retained.

were laid on this road, there was a second line to Chihuahua. Entrance into El Paso was made through a short subsidiary, El Paso Southern Railway, which laid tracks in 1897–98 from Sixth and South Mesa streets to the center of the bridge to meet the MNW Ry. When the MNW was sold to the Mexican government in 1952—it was now part of the Chihuahua al Pacifico—ownership of this line eventually came into the hands of the SP.

Santa Fe located its yards between the present Union Station and the river with the roundhouse situated close to the depot. The Texas and Pacific yard borders on the south side of Overland Avenue while its roundhouse was east of Cotton Avenue.

After the EP&SW took over the EP&NE in 1905, it chose El Paso as the site for its shops and general office building (opened November 1907) to serve both the Eastern and Western Divi-

The eastbound **Golden State** *passes EP&SW locomotive No. 1 in downtown El Paso.*

sions. This meant removal of the EP&NE shops from Alamogordo to the larger quarters at Piedras and Missouri streets, El Paso, in 1907. Following the merger of the EP&SW with the SP in 1924, all work was done at Piedras Street and the shops and the 24-stall roundhouse of the GH&SA at Octavia Street were abandoned, thus permitting expansion of the yard. For many years, the GH&SA (SP) yard had been rimmed on the north by the EP&SW and on the south by the former EP&NE.

Not only was El Paso a commercial supply base for New Mexico, its series of smelters and refineries drew ores and concentrates from New Mexico and adjoining areas. West of El Paso is the large smelter of the American Smelting and Refining Company (formerly the Consolidated Kansas City Smelting and Refining Company) while on the east side is the refinery of Phelps Dodge. To them many thousands of cars have been delivered by the railroads each year.

*El Paso's streetcar system was extensive and remained in oper-
ation long after those in other cities had expired. A typical car of
the El Paso City line is shown here, a city car in the last year of
operation in 1946. (W. C. Whittaker Collection.) Below, two cars
are crossing the Rio Grande bridge into El Paso. The border has
since been moved some 700 feet farther north.*

In November 1923, amid smoke and dust, workmen busily added eight stalls on the west side of the SP (GH&SA) roundhouse in El Paso.

With all the railroads in El Paso, it was not surprising that the need for a union station was recognized as there were almost as many stations scattered about the city as there were railroads. Railroad engineers were busy in the fall of 1901 examining four prospective sites for a union depot. El Paso Union Passenger Depot Company, formed in 1903, was a separate company owned by the railroads. The site selected adjacent to the Rio Grande required much filling for the station grounds on which the brick buildings were built and about three miles of track were laid. Completed in November 1905, the new depot was placed in formal operation March 1, 1906.

El Paso's early physical expansion was largely dictated by the availability of space between Franklin Mountain and the curving Rio Grande. The GH&SA tracks on Main Street and the EP&SW tracks a half block to the north contributed to the

Filling the oil tank at the El Paso roundhouse in 1940. SP No. 4310, designated as a Mountain-1 type, was one of 28 built by Alco in 1924–25.

The Texas and Pacific Railway and the Southern Pacific linked El Paso with East Texas and New Orleans but by different routes. The T&P used locomotives such as No. 718 in its service. A. C. Phelps photograph, 1946.

Mexico Northwestern Railway No. 42 at Juárez in September 1952. This locomotive was purchased from the Missouri-Kansas-Texas Railroad. A. C. Phelps photograph.

congestion of downtown El Paso as it grew in that direction. A solution was not easy but, after considerable negotiations, plans were drawn and an agreement was reached for the sharing of the cost of the $5,000,000 grade-separation project. Through the heart of the city, the former EP&SW tracks were placed in a depression over which eight street crossings were made and the tracks on Main Street were removed. Work began in 1948 and on February 28, 1951 the El Paso (Bataan Memorial) Trainway was placed in operation.

For many years, the location of the United States–Mexican boundary had been confused by the meandering Rio Grande. Incomplete and unsatisfactory settlements had been the order of things until 1962 when the Chamizal Project received serious consideration looking toward a lasting solution. Under the project, the course of the Rio Grande was straightened by building a new channel about 700 feet to the north. Among those affected were the railroads; much of the joint T&P-SP (former EP&NE) track and River (Stanton Street) Yard had to be moved for their underlying land would shortly be in Mexico. As might be expected, much planning and negotiating were necessary in order to relocate the bridges, tracks and yard. Operations in the new River Yard began August 1, 1967 and the new river channel was declared complete December 13, 1968.

Local transportation was essential to the citizens of both countries and mule car lines appeared soon after the arrival of the first steam trains. A group headed by General Anson Mills chartered the El Paso Street Railway Company which began operations in 1882, linking El Paso with Paso del Norte (Juarez) using the Stanton Street bridge. A disruption of service occurred in June 1884 when high water swept away the street car bridge. Undaunted by this catastrophe, the transit company quickly provided temporary service; a boat carried passengers across the river to the waiting cars.

As El Paso grew in size, more mule car lines appeared. The Santa Fe Street Railway Company completed its bridge over the Rio Grande and began service seven years later. Then a series of mergers took place. In 1892, the Santa Fe Street and Juarez Avenue Railway Company and the El Paso and Paso del Norte Street Railway and Bridge Company were consolidated to become El Paso and Juarez Avenue Street Railway, operating

Built as the general office for the EP&SW System, this seven-story building at 416 North Stanton Street served as the SP's El Paso office for many years.

The office of the El Paso Southern Railway was located at the southeast corner of Sixth and Mesa Streets in El Paso. The staff came outside for the photographer on a chilly day in December 1946.

ten cars over 3.5 miles of track with a stable of 50 animals.

In 1901, El Paso Electric Railway was formed, poles were placed along the streets and wires were strung. Amid colorful civic ceremonies the first electric car began operating to Juarez on January 11, 1902. Later that year, when trolleys began running on North Oregon Street, a total of six miles was electrified. In the next few years, electric lines were extended into the residential districts, west to the smelter and east to Fort Bliss. A subsidiary, Rio Grande Valley Traction Company, opened an interurban line to Ysleta on August 30, 1913 (about twelve miles).

At the peak of operations in 1920, El Paso Electric Railway's fleet consisted of 103 cars running over 64 miles of track. Patrons that year numbered 19 million. After that banner year, the use of street cars all over the country declined and those in El Paso suffered along with the others. Ysleta lost its trolleys in November 1925 when seven miles of track were abandoned. To serve new areas, buses were installed in 1926 but the first major substitution was held off until 1929 when buses replaced cars on the smelter line. By 1940 all street car lines had been converted with the exception of the Fort Bliss and (Washington) Park lines in El Paso and the line to Juarez.

On the last day of 1943, El Paso Electric Company, which had for many years held the stock of the El Paso Electric Railway Company and the El Paso and Juarez Traction Company (operating in Mexico), sold these companies to a subsidiary of National City Lines. The bus and street car lines in El Paso were transferred to a new subsidiary, El Paso City Lines, while the corporate status of the Mexican portion remained unchanged.

August 17, 1947 marked the end of street car operation within El Paso when the two remaining lines made their final runs. Passengers on the last trips rode free as they had done the day electric service began 45 years earlier but one lady had the distinction of enjoying a free ride on both the first and last days of the electric car lines. And so the trolley became only a memory in El Paso except for the fabled international line to Juarez for which PCC streamlined cars were purchased. A ride on that line proved an interesting and enjoyable venture for natives and visitors alike.

In an unusually abrupt manner, the operation of the international streetcar ended on July 31, 1973 as the result of a labor dispute. The event had many interesting ramifications and, for a detailed account of this termination of operations, the reader is referred to Thomas J. Price's *Standoff at the Border*, published in 1989 by the Texas Western Press in El Paso.

APPENDIX: SOME NEW MEXICO RAILROAD PASSES

On the following pages are a selection of rare New Mexico railroad passes from the collection of Fred M. Springer. The first two are from a pair of the state's chronically impoverished short lines, the New Mexico Central and the Cimarron & Northwestern. On the following page, three from the EP&NE-EP&SW system (Eddy's "White Oak Route"); and another three from other obscure shortlines—the New Mexico Midland, the St. Louis, Rocky Mountain & Pacific Railway, and the Texas–New Mexico. The final two pages include early examples from several major lines and the short-lived Swastika Route.

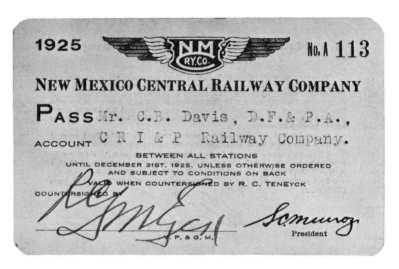

1925 NM RY.CO. No. A 113

NEW MEXICO CENTRAL RAILWAY COMPANY

PASS Mr. C.B. Davis, D.F. & P.A.,

ACCOUNT C R I & P Railway Company.

BETWEEN ALL STATIONS
UNTIL DECEMBER 31ST, 1925, UNLESS OTHERWISE ORDERED
AND SUBJECT TO CONDITIONS ON BACK
VALID WHEN COUNTERSIGNED BY R. C. TENEYCK

COUNTERSIGNED BY

G. P. & G. M.   President

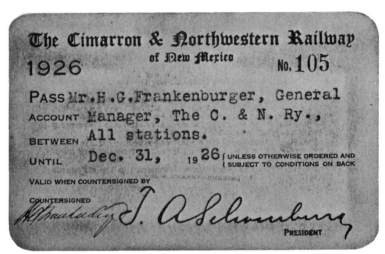

The Cimarron & Northwestern Railway
of New Mexico

1926   No. 105

PASS Mr. H.G. Frankenburger, General

ACCOUNT Manager, The C. & N. Ry.,

BETWEEN All stations.

UNTIL Dec. 31, 19 26 { UNLESS OTHERWISE ORDERED AND SUBJECT TO CONDITIONS ON BACK

VALID WHEN COUNTERSIGNED BY

COUNTERSIGNED

PRESIDENT

Pass ---- J. S. Jones. ----
Sec'y & Auditor. Ft W & R. G. Ry

LUMBER   COAL & COKE
Good on Lines shown on reverse side until Dec. 31 unless sooner revoked.
Nº A 408
PRESIDENT

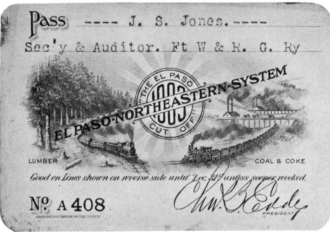

Pass   J. S. Jones,
Secty. & Audr. F.W & R.G. Ry.

LUMBER   COAL & COKE
Good on Lines shown on reverse side until Dec. 31 unless sooner revoked.
Nº A 501
PRESIDENT

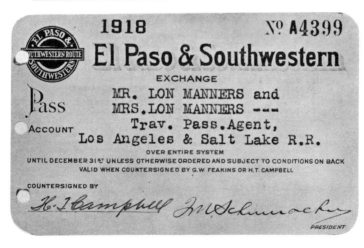

1918   Nº A4399
El Paso & Southwestern
EXCHANGE

Pass   MR. LON MANNERS and
          MRS. LON MANNERS ---
Account   Trav. Pass. Agent,
        Los Angeles & Salt Lake R.R.
OVER ENTIRE SYSTEM
UNTIL DECEMBER 31ST UNLESS OTHERWISE ORDERED AND SUBJECT TO CONDITIONS ON BACK
VALID WHEN COUNTERSIGNED BY G.W. FEAKINS OR H.T. CAMPBELL

COUNTERSIGNED BY
H.T. Campbell   F.N. Schumacher
                              PRESIDENT

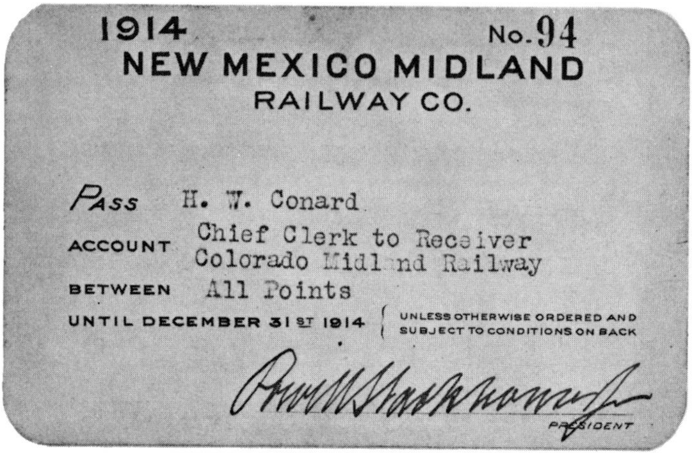

1914 No. 94
NEW MEXICO MIDLAND
RAILWAY CO.

Pass H. W. Conard
ACCOUNT Chief Clerk to Receiver
Colorado Midland Railway
BETWEEN All Points
UNTIL DECEMBER 31ST 1914 { UNLESS OTHERWISE ORDERED AND
SUBJECT TO CONDITIONS ON BACK

PRESIDENT

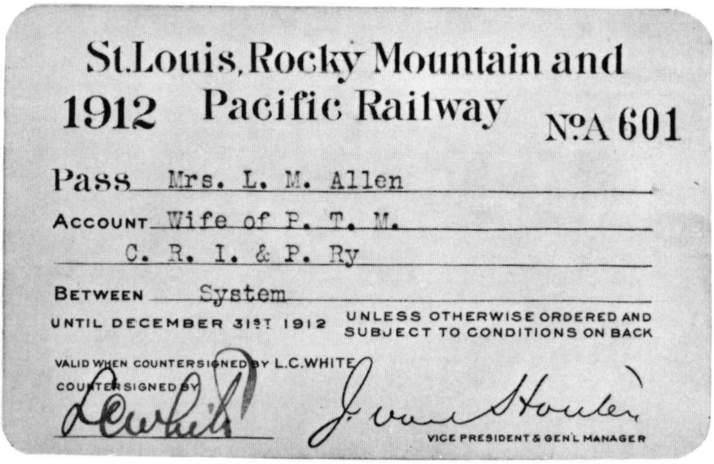

St. Louis, Rocky Mountain and
1912 Pacific Railway N°A 601

Pass Mrs. L. M. Allen
Account Wife of P. T. M.
C. R. I. & P. Ry
BETWEEN System
UNTIL DECEMBER 31ST 1912 UNLESS OTHERWISE ORDERED AND
SUBJECT TO CONDITIONS ON BACK
VALID WHEN COUNTERSIGNED BY L.C. WHITE
COUNTERSIGNED BY

VICE PRESIDENT & GEN'L MANAGER

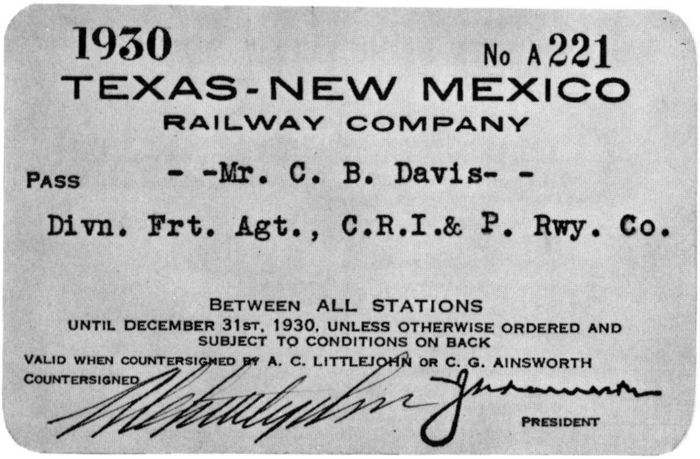

1930 No A 221
TEXAS-NEW MEXICO
RAILWAY COMPANY

PASS - -Mr. C. B. Davis- -

Divn. Frt. Agt., C.R.I.& P. Rwy. Co.

BETWEEN ALL STATIONS
UNTIL DECEMBER 31ST, 1930, UNLESS OTHERWISE ORDERED AND
SUBJECT TO CONDITIONS ON BACK
VALID WHEN COUNTERSIGNED BY A. C. LITTLEJOHN OR C. G. AINSWORTH
COUNTERSIGNED

PRESIDENT

St. Louis, Rocky Mountain and Pacific Railway
1911 NºA 585

Pass J. E. Gorman, car & Ry. Employees,

Account Vice-Pres. Rock Island Lines.

UNTIL DECEMBER 31ST 1911 { UNLESS OTHERWISE ORDERED AND SUBJECT TO CONDITIONS ON BACK

VALID WHEN COUNTERSIGNED BY L.C. WHITE

COUNTERSIGNED BY

VICE PRESIDENT & GEN'L MANAGER

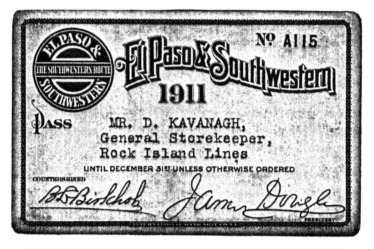

El Paso & Southwestern
Nº A115
1911

PASS MR. D. KAVANAGH,
General Storekeeper,
Rock Island Lines

UNTIL DECEMBER 31ST UNLESS OTHERWISE ORDERED

COUNTERSIGNED

PRESIDENT

1917 Nº 222
El Paso & Southwestern

Pass MR. J. E. GORMAN, Chf. Ex. Officer,
Account Car, Five Officers & Employes,
C. R. I. & P. Railway

OVER ENTIRE SYSTEM

UNTIL DECEMBER 31ST UNLESS OTHERWISE ORDERED AND SUBJECT TO CONDITIONS ON BACK

VICE-PRESIDENT

INDEX

White Oaks, N.M., 71, 73, 78, 84, 156

White Oaks Canyon, 86

White Oaks Route, 257, 259

White Pine Lumber Co., 228, 230

White Rock Cañon, 110, 117, 224

Whitewater, N.M., 186, 193

Whitney, J. Parker, 193

Whitney Junction, 198

Willard, N.M., 58

Willis Canyon, 220

Willow Creek, 208

Willow Springs, N.M., 5

Wilson Mesa, N.M., 223

Wink, Texas, 151, 153

Wink Junction, 153

Wootton, "Uncle Dick," 2, 4

X.I.T. Ranch, 143

Yankee, N.M., 163, 165

Yankee coal mine, 159, 163

Yankee Fuel Co., 163

York Canyon, N.M., 156, 165, 166, 168

Ysleta, Texas, 255, 256

Yuma, Ariz., xiv, 8, 60

Zimmerman, George, 213

Zora, N.M., 100

Zuni Canyon, 213

Zuni Indians, 211

Zuni Mountain RR., 209–15

Zuni Mountains, 209, 214, 220, 223, 237